Lecture Notes in Computer Science 4440

Commenced Publication in 1973
Founding and Former Series Editors:
Gerhard Goos, Juris Hartmanis, and Jan van Leeuwen

Editorial Board

Ben Liblit

Cooperative Bug Isolation

Winning Thesis of the
2005 ACM Doctoral Dissertation Competition

 Springer

Author

Ben Liblit
University of Wisconsin–Madison
Computer Sciences Department
1210 West Dayton Street, Madison, WI 53706-1685, USA
E-mail: liblit@cs.wisc.edu

Library of Congress Control Number: 2007924082

CR Subject Classification (1998): D.2.4-5, D.2.2, F.3, F.2.2, I.2.8

LNCS Sublibrary: SL 2 – Programming and Software Engineering

ISSN   0302-9743
ISBN-10   3-540-71877-X Springer Berlin Heidelberg New York
ISBN-13   978-3-540-71877-2 Springer Berlin Heidelberg New York

Springer is a part of Springer Science+Business Media

springer.com

© Springer-Verlag Berlin Heidelberg 2007

Typesetting: Camera-ready by author, data conversion by Markus Richter, Heidelberg
Printed on acid-free paper   SPIN: 12046706   06/3180   5 4 3 2 1 0

*To my parents, for their unwavering love and
support throughout this and all my adventures*

Foreword

Efforts to understand and predict the behavior of software date back to the earliest days of computer programming, over half a century ago. In the intervening decades, the need for effective methods of understanding software has only increased; software has spread to become the underpinning of much of modern society, and the potentially disastrous consequences of broken or poorly understood software have become all too apparent. Ben Liblit's work reconsiders two common assumptions about how we should analyze software and it arrives at some striking new results.

In principle, understanding software is not such a hard problem. Certainly a computer scientist studying programs appears to be in a much stronger position than, say, a biologist trying to understand a living organism or an economist trying to understand the behavior of markets, because the biologist and the economist must rely on indirect observation of the basic processes they wish to understand. A computer scientist, however, starts with a complete, precise description of the behavior of software—the program itself! Of course, the story turns out not to be so straightforward, because despite having a perfect description, programs are sufficiently complex that it is usually difficult or even impossible to answer many simple questions about them. Ben's first change of assumption comes from the observation that if programs are hard to understand, perhaps we could make use of some of the tools that biologists and economists use to understand their complicated systems: maybe it would be productive to regard programs as statistical processes and use statistical techniques to understand software. We can simply run the program, make some observations and, if we ask the right questions, learn something useful about program behavior. What questions to ask, and how to answer them, is the topic of the second half of this book.

The second key ingredient comes from asking the question: Which program runs should we use to gather the observations? Using test cases or automatically synthesized inputs is a bit unsatisfying, as these executions may not be representative of the reality of what users do with the software. And therein lies the answer: Use the runs of the program's users. These runs define the reality of how the software behaves in practice; in a real sense, these are the executions that matter. In a networked world it is possible to gather a small amount of information from every execution ever performed and from that information build up a model of program behavior about which statistically meaningful statements can be made. How to actually gather that information in a way that is unobtrusive and efficient as well as statistically sound is the subject of the first half of this book.

The centerpiece of the monograph is an algorithm for isolating multiple bugs from sparsely sampled data taken from many thousands of program executions. The basic idea is to see which program events are strongly correlated with a subset of program failures, remove those failures from consideration and then, recursively, compute what events are correlated with the remaining failures. This algorithm has unique properties that complement other program analysis techniques; in particular, it is potentially able to find the root cause of any program failure without first requiring an explicit specification of the property to check. While Ben's work focuses on finding the causes of bugs, the underlying approach is much more general and should be adaptable to any program-understanding problem where one wants to discover which program events are strongly correlated with some observable behavior. The results Ben presents represent a new and fundamental approach to software analysis and should provide a source of ideas and inspiration to the field for many years to come.

January 2007   Alex Aiken

Preface

This book contains a revised version of the dissertation the author wrote in the Computer Science Division of the Department of Electrical Engineering and Computer Science of the University of California, Berkeley. The dissertation was submitted to the Graduate Division in conformity with the requirements for the degree of Doctor of Philosophy in December 2004. It was honored with the 2005 ACM Doctoral Dissertation Award in May 2005.

Abstract

Debugging does not end with deployment. Static analysis, in-house testing, and good software engineering practices can catch or prevent many problems before software is distributed. Yet mainstream commercial software still ships with both known and unknown bugs. Real software still fails in the hands of real users. The need remains to identify and repair bugs that are only discovered, or whose importance is only revealed, after the software is released. Unfortunately, we know almost nothing about how software behaves (and misbehaves) in the hands of end users. Traditional post-deployment feedback mechanisms, such as technical support phone calls or hand-composed bug reports, are informal, inconsistent, and highly dependent on manual, human intervention. This approach clouds the view, preventing engineers from seeing a complete and truly representative picture of how and why problems occur.

This book proposes a system to support debugging based on feedback from actual users. *Cooperative Bug Isolation* (CBI) leverages the key strength of user communities: their overwhelming numbers. We propose a low-overhead instrumentation strategy for gathering information from the executions experienced by large numbers of software end users. Our approach limits overhead using sparse random sampling rather than complete data collection, while simultaneously ensuring that the observed data is an unbiased, representative subset of the complete program behavior across all runs. We discuss a number of specific instrumentation schemes that may be coupled with the general sampling transformation to produce feedback data that we have found to be useful for isolating the causes of a wide variety of bugs.

Collecting feedback from real code, especially real buggy code, is a nontrivial exercise. This book presents our approach to a number of practical challenges that arise in building a complete, working CBI system. We discuss how the general sampling transformation scheme can be extended to deal with native compilers, libraries, dynamically loaded code, threads, and other features of modern software. We address questions of privacy and security as well as related issues of user interaction and informed user consent. This design and engineering investment has allowed us to begin an actual public deployment of a CBI system, initial results from which we report here.

Of course, feedback data is only as useful as the sense we can make of it. When data is fair but very sparse, the noise level is high and traditional manual debugging techniques insufficient. This book presents a suite of new algorithms for *statistical debugging*: finding and fixing software errors based on statistical analysis of sparse feedback data. The techniques vary in complexity and sophistication, from simple process of elimination strategies to regression techniques that build models of suspect program behaviors as failure predictors. Our most advanced technique combines a number of general and domain-specific statistical filtering and ranking techniques to separate the effects of different bugs and identify predictors that are associated with individual bugs. These predictors reveal both the circumstances under which bugs occur and the frequencies of failure modes, making it easier to prioritize debugging efforts. Our algorithm is validated using several case studies. These case studies include examples in which the algorithm found previously unknown, significant crashing bugs in widely used systems.

Acknowledgments

First and foremost, I wish to thank my advisor Alex Aiken. The best way I know to show my gratitude is to aspire to be for my students what Alex has been for me: teacher, collaborator, mentor, guide ... role model.

Alice Zheng has been my statistically minded other half in what has evolved into a deeply rewarding cross-disciplinary collaboration. Thank you, Alice. I couldn't have done it without you.

This project has easily produced ten bad ideas for every good one. Michael Jordan met all of our brainstorming with patient explanations and unmatched expertise. It has been a pleasure and an honor having Mike on the team.

Mayur Naik's creativity, energy, and seemingly boundless enthusiasm have made him a delight to work with. Mayur, it's been great fun just trying to keep up with you.

The path balancing optimization is based on ideas first suggested by Cormac Flanagan.

This research began under the auspices of the Open Source Quality Project, whose faculty, student, and staff members have been a valuable source of insight and inspiration over the years. Special thanks are due to George Necula and his students for creating and maintaining the CIL C front end upon which our instrumentor is based.

I am indebted to the many members of the open source community who have supported our work. My thanks go out to the many anonymous users of our public deployment, and to the developers of the open source projects used in our public deployment and case studies. I am especially grateful to Luis Villa, Jody Goldberg, and Colin Walters for their longstanding interest in and encouragement of this research.

While conducting this research, my collaborators and I were supported in part by DARPA ARO-MURI ACCLIMATE DAAD-19-02-1-0383; DOE Prime Contract No. W-7405-ENG-48 through Memorandum Agreement No. B504962 with LLNL; NASA Grant No. NAG2-1210; NSF Grant Nos. EIA-9802069, CCR-0085949, ACI-9619020, and IIS-9988642; ONR MURI Grant N00014-00-1-0637; a grant from Microsoft Research; and a Lucent GRPW Fellowship.

January 2007   Ben Liblit

Contents

1

Introduction

There are no significant bugs in our released software that any significant number of users want fixed.

–Bill Gates quoted in Focus *Magazine*

Real software is buggy. Real users can make it better. Cooperative Bug Isolation (*CBI*) seeks to leverage the huge amount of computation done by the end users of software. By gathering a little bit of information from every run of a program performed by its user community, we are able to make inferences automatically about the causes of bugs encountered in the field.

1.1 Perfect, or Close Enough

Many computer scientists think of a program as either correct (i.e., it meets some specification) or incorrect (i.e., it does not meet some specification). But industrial software development is as much about economics as computer science. Software quality is a monetary balancing act among engineers' salaries, time to market, user expectations, and other business concerns. We ship software when it seems correct enough to neither embarrass us nor alienate users. We ship software with known bugs that are not worth fixing, and users uncover new bugs that developers never imagined. An observer in residence at the game development studios of Electronic Arts (EA) wrote that

> The largest sin at EA is not delivering a title on time. ... Making an outstanding game, but delivering it late, is not as profitable as making an acceptable quality game on time. EAers talk about "maximum on-time-quality." [52]

Clearly practitioners use something other than a Boolean notion of correctness, but such a notion has been difficult to quantify. In-house testing can only guess at field usage patterns, and poor guesses can leave users in bad shape. A seemingly obscure, low-priority bug that was difficult to reproduce in the testing lab may turn out to affect large numbers of users on a regular basis. Technical support channels provide one way for post-deployment feedback to reach engineers, but traditionally these mechanisms have been informal and overly dependent on human intervention.

B. Liblit: Cooperative Bug Isolation, LNCS 4440, pp. 1–6, 2007.
© Springer-Verlag Berlin Heidelberg 2007

1.2 Automatic Failure Reporting

Industry critics have said that many software vendors treat their customers like beta testers. If that is so, then we are not yet using these thousands or millions of testers as effectively as we could. Traditionally, most software failures produce a grumpy user and no diagnostic feedback, which benefits no one.

This situation is starting to change as a result of ubiquitous Internet connectivity. KDE, GNOME, Mozilla/Netscape, and Microsoft have all deployed automated, opt-in crash reporting systems. These systems gather key information about program state after a failure has occurred: stack trace, register contents, and the like. By sending this information back to the development organization, the user community helps developers effectively triage bugs that cause crashes and focus on the problems experienced by the most users.

However, automatic crash reporting systems create a new problem: developers who are overwhelmed with bug reports, many of which may be redundant, and who must prioritize their work in terms of which bug fixes are likely to provide the greatest net benefit in the shortest amount of time. As of this writing, the Bugzilla bug tracking database for the open source Mozilla web browser project shows 58,661 open bugs; an additional 104,764 have been marked as duplicates of bugs already reported [44]. Mozilla augments manual bug reporting with an automated crash feedback system. This system currently shows 186,180 automated crash reports for Mozilla Firefox 2.0 over a ten day period, accounting for 5,024,104 hours of "testing" by end users [45]. As early as 2002, Microsoft's Watson error reporting service had collected crash reports from half a million separate programs. Experience with Watson has shown that one percent of software errors cause fifty percent of user crashes [41].

We believe that ubiquitous crash reporting is progress in the right direction, but we also believe that existing approaches only scratch the surface of what is possible when developers and users are connected by a network. For example, crash reporting systems in mainstream end user environments do not gather any information about what happened before the crash. Trace information leading up to the failure may contain critical clues to the actual problem. Also, crash reporting systems report no information for successful runs, which makes it difficult to distinguish anomalous (crash-causing) behavior from innocuous behavior common to all executions. In general, the information gathered by crash reporting systems is not very systematic, and in all feedback systems of which we are aware (crash reporting or otherwise) the subsequent data analysis is highly manual.

1.3 The Next Step Forward

The high level of redundancy exhibited by existing crash reporting systems suggests that there is great potential to harness the user community as a distributed, brute force bug hunting resource. Because the most important bugs are those that happen most often to the most users, it is not necessary to trace program behavior in a complete, invasive, perfectly controlled manner. Rather, we can use lightweight instrumentation to sample a small amount of information about each run, and then merge this information to form an aggregate picture of how the software is working and failing in the field. Furthermore, the feedback loop can flow in both directions: aggregate error reporting can direct engineers toward bugs, and engineers can steer instrumentation toward code regions of interest based on observed failure trends.

The idea of gathering data from actual user executions is not new. Large enterprise database systems, for example, routinely produce extensive log files. The first action when a user reports a problem is to inspect those logs. Similarly, each flight of the Boeing 777 generates logs that are subsequently combed for signs of possible problems [21]. There are many other similar examples in the world of high end and safety critical systems. However, no such feedback channels have been available to the multitudinous end users of mainstream commercial software.

In our view, wide deployment of such an infrastructure would have several benefits:

- For deployed software systems, the number of executions in actual use dwarfs the number of executions produced in testing by orders of magnitude. For many software systems today, essentially all of the information from user executions is discarded, because there is no mechanism for feedback. Retaining even a small portion of that information could be valuable.
- Gathering information from all, or at least a representative sample, of user executions gives an accurate picture of how the software is actually used, allowing better decisions about how to spend scarce resources on modifications. In particular, bugs that affect a large number of users are a higher priority than bugs that are very rare. This kind of information is almost impossible to obtain from anywhere other than actual user executions.
- While our primary interest is in finding and fixing quality problems, information gathered from user executions could be useful for other purposes. For example, software authors may simply wish to know which features are most commonly used, or we may be interested in discovering whether code not covered by in-house testing is ever executed in practice, etc.
- Traditional user feedback about problems often consists of a call from a relatively unsophisticated user to a perhaps only somewhat more sophisticated technical support center. In a networked world, it is simply more efficient and accurate to gather this information automatically.
- Many bugs sit on open bug lists of products for an extended period of time before an engineer is available to work on the bug. Automatically gathering data from user executions allows for automated analysis without human intervention. Thus, when an engineer is finally available to work on a problem, the results of automated analyses done in the interim may help the engineer to identify and fix even relatively simple problems more quickly.

1.4 Cooperative Bug Isolation

A Cooperative Bug Isolation system must meet several challenges if it is to be viable in the real world. The first problem is that the method for gathering information must have only a modest impact on the performance of the user's program. Our approach, discussed in Chap. 2, is based on fair random sampling. Classical sampling for measuring program performance searches for the "elephant in the haystack": it is looking for the biggest consumers of time. In contrast, we are looking for needles (bugs) that may occur very rarely, and furthermore our sampling rates may be very low to maintain client performance. These requirements lead us to be concerned with guaranteeing that the sampling is statistically fair, so that we can rely on the reported frequencies of rare events. Chapter 2 presents a general sampling transformation, applied at compile time, that converts unconditional instrumentation into instrumentation that is sampled randomly but fairly, in a very strict statistical sense, as the program runs.

A second problem is that information from the client must be transmitted over the network to a central database. Gathering even a relatively small amount of data periodically from a large number of clients creates significant scalability problems. One would like to monitor behaviors that are likely to be probative regarding a wide variety of yet-unknown bugs while still reducing, compacting, or even discarding enough information to keep communication and storage requirements modest. Chapter 2 continues with a discussion of several instrumentation schemes that we find to be scalable and useful in practice for distributed debugging. The remainder of Chap. 2 explores additional performance optimizations and variations on the basic sampling strategy.

A third, perhaps more vague problem is that such a system must actually work with real applications, on real desktops, in the hands of real users. Chapter 3 discusses our solutions to a potpourri of issues that arise in assembling a complete, working Cooperative Bug Isolation system. We discuss how the transformations of Chap. 2 interact with features of various modern languages and software architectures; consider privacy and security concerns and steps taken to address them; present a view of the system from the end user's perspective; and conclude the chapter with a review of the status of a large scale public deployment of Cooperative Bug Isolation that is currently under way.

The fourth and ultimate challenge is using this randomly sampled, noisy, terribly incomplete data to actually find and fix bugs. Why do some runs succeed and others fail? How does the sparsely observed behavior of good runs differ from that in bad runs? Our strategy for answering these questions, *statistical debugging*, is based on building statistical models of program success or failure as a function of observed behaviors. Chapter 4 describes several statistical debugging techniques that we have developed from the simple to the sophisticated. We present the results of several case studies used to evaluate our statistical debugging algorithms.

Figure 1.1 presents an informal, conceptual overview of our system showing how its pieces fit together to form a feedback loop of continuously improving software quality.

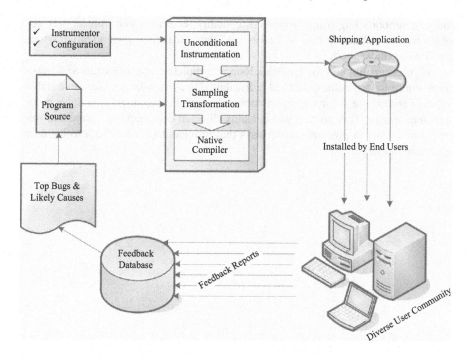

Fig. 1.1. Conceptual overview of Cooperative Bug Isolation system

The process begins at left, with program source. Our system requires no manual instrumentation or annotation: we work directly with unmodified C code. We feel that this design constraint was important to facilitate rapid adoption by large, pre-existing application code bases. Program source is fed into a tool chain that appears from the outside to be a standard compiler augmented with some additional high-level configuration options. Internally, however, the build process has three distinct steps: insertion of unconditional instrumentation, generic sampling transformation, then native compilation to binaries ready for distribution.

End users install the shipping application, thereby forming a large, diverse user community. Each use of an application, whether successful or failed, generates a feedback report. The feedback report consists of a concise instrumentation dump along with a binary outcome flag: did the run succeed or fail? "Fail" here might simply be defined as "crashed," as crashing is an easy outcome to detect and something that we all agree should never happen. However, one of our case studies demonstrates that more refined, domain-specific notions of failure are equally viable. All we require is a binary outcome label.

A central feedback database aggregates these feedback reports for analysis. Using statistical debugging techniques, we identify those behaviors that are strongly correlated with failure along with information about how often the various failure modes occur. This information helps engineers fix individual bugs. Just as importantly, it supports bug triage grounded in reality: engineers can immediately see which bugs are affecting the most users, and thus focus their own attention where it will do the most good.

As engineers fix bugs the feedback loop is completed. Improvements to the program source are re-instrumented and redistributed to users, who now see more stable software and whose feedback reports now focus even more sharply on those problems that remain. This process yields reality-directed debugging: software that improves over time in precisely those ways that provide the most benefit to the user community at large.

2

Instrumentation Framework

> *The major difference between a thing that might go wrong and*
> *a thing that cannot possibly go wrong is that when a thing that*
> *cannot possibly go wrong goes wrong, it usually turns out to*
> *be impossible to get at or repair.*

> *–Douglas Adams,* Mostly Harmless

This chapter describes the process of going from unmodified application source code to native executables with sampled instrumentation. This process is managed by the *instrumentor*: a software tool whose external behavior mimics that of the native compiler, but that internally applies the instrumentation injection and sampling transformation steps depicted at the top center of Fig. 1.1. Our instrumentor, `sampler-cc`, is implemented as a source-to-source transformation for C using the CIL C front end [48]. Transformed code then proceeds to GCC for native compilation. From the developer's perspective, the `sampler-cc` command behaves exactly like the `gcc` command with a few extra instrumentation-related command line flags.

Section 2.1 presents the basic strategy for managing fair, randomly sampled instrumentation. This sampling transformation is quite general, with potential applications beyond bug hunting. However, bug hunting is the focus of this book, and Sect. 2.2 describes several instrumentation schemes that may be used with the sampling transformation and that we have found to be helpful for bug isolation. Section 2.3 considers performance issues and examines several optimizations that may be applied atop the basic sampling transformation. Section 2.4 describes an adaptive, non-uniformly sampled generalization of the core random sampling model, while Sect. 2.5 closes the chapter with an informal discussion of realistic sampling rates in truly large scale deployments.

2.1 Basic Instrumentation Strategy

This section describes our sampling framework. We begin with sampling of basic blocks and gradually add features until we can describe how to perform sampling for entire programs. Suppose we start with the following C code:

```
{
    check(p != NULL);
    p = p->next;
```

B. Liblit: Cooperative Bug Isolation, LNCS 4440, pp. 7–38, 2007.
© Springer-Verlag Berlin Heidelberg 2007

```
    check(i < max);
    total += sizes[i];
}
```

Our sampling framework can be configured to sample arbitrary pieces of code, which may be either portions of the original program or instrumentation predicates added separately. Section 2.2 describes several instrumentation schemes that we have found useful. For the remainder of this section, assume that each italicized *check* call is an instrumentation site that has been tagged for sampling. The precise behavior of an instrumentation site is of no concern to the sampling transformation itself. We require only that each such site be removable. That is, performing some *check* calls and skipping others must not affect the user-visible behavior of the program.

2.1.1 Sampling the Bernoulli Way

Suppose that we wish to sample one hundredth of these checks. Maintaining a global counter modulo one hundred is simple, but has the disadvantage of being trivially periodic. If the above fragment were in a loop, for example, one of the checks would execute on every fiftieth iteration while the other would never execute. To avoid this temporal aliasing we wish sampling to be fair and uniformly random: each check should independently have a $1/100$ chance of being sampled each time it occurs. This property is characteristic of a so-called *Bernoulli process*, the most common example of which is repeatedly tossing a coin. We wish to sample based on the outcome of tossing a coin that is biased to come up heads only one time in a hundred.

A naïve approach would be to use a simple random number generator. Suppose $rnd(n)$ yields a random integer uniformly distributed between 0 and $n-1$. Then the following code gives us fair random sampling at the desired density:

```
{
    if (rnd(100) == 0) check(p != NULL);
    p = p->next;

    if (rnd(100) == 0) check(i < max);
    total += sizes[i];
}
```

This strategy has some practical problems. Random number generation is not free: tossing the coin may be slower than simply doing the check unconditionally. Furthermore, what was previously straight-line code is now dense with branches and joins, which may impede other optimizations.

Sampling is sparse. Each of the conditionals has a $99/100 = 99\%$ chance of not sampling. On any run through this block, there is a $(99/100)^2 \approx 98\%$ chance that both instrumentation sites are skipped. If we determine, upon reaching the top of a basic block, that no site in that block is sampled, then we can branch into fast-path code with all conditionally-guarded checks removed. This design requires two versions of the code: one with sampled instrumentation, one without. It also requires that we can predict how many future sampling opportunities are skipped before the next one is taken.

Anticipating future samples requires a change in randomization strategy. Consider a sequence of biased coin tosses, with "0" indicating no sample and "1" indicating that a sample is to be taken. Temporarily increasing the sampling density to $\frac{1}{5}$, we might have:

$$\underbrace{\langle 0,0,0,0,0,1,}_{6} \underbrace{0,0,0,1,}_{4} \underbrace{0,1,}_{2} \underbrace{0,0,1,}_{3} \ldots \rangle$$

An equivalent representation counts the number of tosses until (and including) the next sampled check: $\langle 6,4,2,3,\ldots \rangle$. This representation is predictive: the head of the sequence can be treated as a countdown, telling us how far away the next sample is. If we are at the top of a basic block containing only two checks, and the next sampling countdown is 6, we know in advance that neither of those sites is sampled on this visit. Instead, we merely discard two tosses and proceed directly to the instrumentation-free fast path:

```
{
    if (countdown > 2) {
        /* fast path: no sample ahead */
        countdown -= 2;
        p = p->next;
        total += sizes[i];
    } else {
        /* slow path: sample is imminent */
        if (--countdown == 0) {
            check(p != NULL);
            countdown = getNextCountdown();
        }
        p = p->next;

        if (--countdown == 0) {
            check(i < max);
            countdown = getNextCountdown();
        }
        total += sizes[i];
    }
}
```

The instrumented code does extra work to manage the next-sample countdown, but the fast path is much improved. The only overhead is a single compare/branch and a constant decrement, and this overhead is amortized over the entire block. In larger blocks with more instrumentation sites, the initial countdown check has a larger threshold, but that one check suffices to predict a larger number of skipped sampling opportunities.

Consider the distribution of countdown values. With a sampling density of $1/100$, there is a $1/100$ chance that we sample at the very next opportunity. There is a $(99/100) \times (1/100)$ that the next chance is skipped but that the one after that is taken. A countdown of three appears on a $(99/100)^2 \times (1/100)$ chance, and so on. These numbers form a *geometric distribution* whose mean value is the inverse of the sampling density (that is, 100). Numbers in a geometric distribution characterize the expected inter-arrival times of a Bernoulli process, such as the number of tails before the next head, or in our case the number of instrumentation sites skipped before the next sample is taken.

Happily, repeated tossing of a biased coin is not necessary: geometrically distributed random numbers can be generated directly using a standard uniform random generator and some simple floating-point operations. Let $rand(0, 1)$ be a source of random floating point numbers on the open interval between zero and one. Let $1/d$ be the desired sampling rate, such as $1/100$. Then a new geometrically distributed countdown may be computed as

$$countdown = \left\lfloor \frac{\log(rand(0, 1))}{\log(1 - 1/d)} \right\rfloor + 1.$$

The denominator in the above equation is fixed for a given sampling rate, so generating one new countdown requires

- one random floating point number
  - m random bits for a floating point representation with an m-bit mantissa
  - discard and repeat if all m bits are 0 (exceedingly rare)
- one floating point logarithm
- one floating point division
- one truncating conversion from floating point to integer
- one integer increment

This work is then amortized across an average of d succeeding instrumentation sites. Subsection 2.3.5 considers additional options for speeding up countdown resets.

In theory, a countdown may need to be arbitrarily large. However, the odds of a $1/100$ countdown exceeding $2^{32} - 1$ are less than one in 10^{10^7}, so storing countdowns as simple 32-bit unsigned integers is sufficient for all practical scenarios.

2.1.2 From Blocks to Functions

The scheme for blocks outlined above generalizes to an arbitrary control flow graph as follows. Any region of acyclic code has a finite number of possible paths. Let the maximum number of instrumented sites on any path be the region's *weight*. A countdown threshold check can be placed at the top of each acyclic region. If the next-sample countdown exceeds the weight of an acyclic region on entry to that region, then no samples are taken on that pass through the region.

Any cycle in a control-flow graph without instrumentation is weightless and may be disregarded. Any cycle with instrumentation must also contain a threshold check, which guarantees that if we start at any threshold check and execute forward, we cross only a statically bounded number of instrumentation sites before reaching the next threshold check. Thus, we can compute a static weight for each threshold check.

There is some flexibility regarding exactly where a threshold check is placed, but computing an optimal solution is NP-hard [32]. For simplicity, our present system places one threshold check at function entry and one along each loop back edge. Weights may be computed in a single bottom-up traversal of each function's control flow graph.

The sampling transformation produces two complete copies of the function body. One contains full instrumentation, with each possible sample guarded by a decrement and test of the next-sample countdown. The other copy, the fast path, merely decrements the countdown where appropriate, but otherwise has all instrumentation removed. We stitch the two variants together at threshold check points: at the top of each acyclic region, we decide whether a sample is imminent. If it is, we branch into the instrumented code. If the next sample is far off, we continue in the fast path code instead.

Figure 2.1 shows an example of code layout for a function containing one conditional and one loop. Dotted nodes represent instrumentation sites; these are reduced to countdown decrements in the fast path. The boxed nodes represent threshold checks; we have added one at function entry and one along the back edge of the loop. This code layout strategy is a variation on that used by Arnold and Ryder to reduce the cost of code instrumented for performance profiling [2]. The principal change in our transformation is the use of geometrically distributed countdowns in conjunction with acyclic region weights to choose between the two code variants. Arnold and Ryder use fixed sampling periods (e.g., exactly once per n opportunities, or exactly once per n instructions) and do not apply region-specific weighting. Our approach imposes more overhead, but offers greater statistical rigor in the resultant sampled data. Arnold and Ryder have studied several variations with different trade-offs of code size versus overhead; the same choices apply here.

2.1.3 Interprocedural Issues

In general, a called function might cross any number of instrumentation sites before returning to its caller. Barring interprocedural analysis, we cannot assign a statically bounded weight to any control flow graph node containing a function call. Therefore, we treat each such call as an acyclic region boundary. A region ends before an opaque function call, and a new region begins just after.

The same treatment applies to language-specific mechanisms for interprocedural control transfer. In C, setjmp and a few related functions form region boundaries. In languages with more structured exception handling, such as Java or C++, a new region forms below the catch point that receives a thrown exception.

If interprocedural analysis is available, then we can avoid splitting regions at some calls. Subsection 2.3.2 discusses this optimization in greater detail.

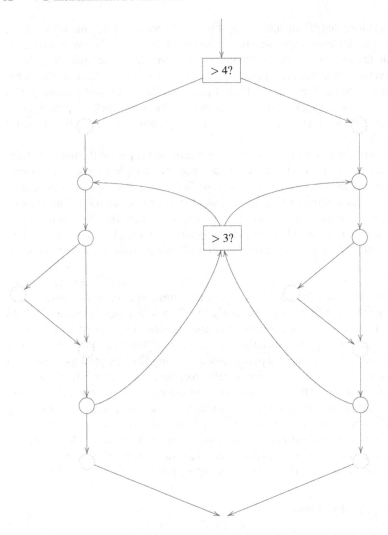

Fig. 2.1. Example of instrumented code layout

2.2 Instrumentation Schemes for Distributed Debugging

Our framework for statistically fair sampling can be used for any program monitoring application. Before examining performance and optimizations in detail, it is useful to have specific scenarios in mind. Our primary interest here is distributed debugging, so we are interested in data that helps engineers find bugs in deployed software. Here we briefly discuss the main problems that arise in this context and a particular solution that we adopt. We then present a suite of instrumentation schemes. These schemes are the basis for the performance and optimization studies that follow, and are also used in several case studies discussed in Chap. 4.

2.2.1 Issues in Remote Sampling

Remote monitoring can harm performance in several ways. As usual the performance penalty imposed by the extra monitoring code cannot be excessive. Disk and memory space is limited, so we must limit the size of data retained, even temporarily, on a user's machine. Network bandwidth to transmit results to a central server is also a concern. The user's primary goal is to use the software, not fix it, so in each of these cases we must be frugal with the user's resources. Any central server has limited storage and communication resources as well, compounded by the fact that it is aggregating many runs. For example, if we wish to retain all sampled data, then storage on the central server grows linearly with the number of executions even if the data collected from each execution is constant size.

Our approach is to sample the value of each of a very large, but fixed, set of predicates on program state. Some predicates are observed directly at instrumentation sites: we call these *fundamental predicates*. In general one instrumentation site may induce multiple predicates at the same location. For example,

"$x < y$ on line 319 of `utils.c`",
"$x = y$ on line 319 of `utils.c`", and
"$x > y$ on line 319 of `utils.c`"

might be three fundamental predicates comparing the values of two variables at a particular instrumentation site. When an observation is made at a site, all fundamental predicates are observed simultaneously. Thus, a single observation of this site appearing on line 319 of `utils.c` would observe one of the three predicates to be true and would observe the other two predicates to be false.

We do not report a running stream of true/false predicate observations as execution proceeds. Rather we only count the *number* of times each fundamental predicate is observed to be true. One global variable maintains the count for each fundamental predicate. We refer to these global variables as *predicate counters* or as simply *counters*. They should not be confused with the global next-sample countdown.

At the end of execution, all counters are serialized into a feedback report giving the final count for each fundamental predicate. For example, we might find that on a particular run,

"$x < y$ on line 319 of `utils.c`" was observed true 25 times,
"$x = y$ on line 319 of `utils.c`" was observed true 3 times, and
"$x > y$ on line 319 of `utils.c`" was observed true 1 time.

We can never know how often the predicates were actually true, but we count how often they were observed to be true.

Maintaining a vector of global counters produces feedback reports whose size is largely independent of the sampling density or running time. The loss of information is significant, as the order of the observations is discarded. However, predicate counters do provide at least a partial window into dynamic program behavior before a failure. That may be a useful addition to the postmortem stack trace commonly used to report fatal errors today.

In some instrumentation schemes, the fundamental predicates can be augmented by a set of *inferred predicates* derived offline. For each inferred predicate we derive an inferred predicate counter that describes how often the inferred predicate would have been observed to be true if it had actually been tracked during execution. Continuing the example from the preceding paragraph, we infer that

"$x \geq y$ on line 319 of `utils.c`" would have been observed true $3 + 1$ times,
"$x \neq y$ on line 319 of `utils.c`" would have been observed true $25 + 1$ times, and
"$x \leq y$ on line 319 of `utils.c`" would have been observed true $25 + 3$ times.

Inferred predicates have no runtime cost and can be particularly useful for distinguishing certain boundary cases, such as $x < y$ versus $x \leq y$. However, they also significantly enlarge the set of possible bug causes, making scalability of bug isolation algorithms more of a concern. The statistical debugging algorithms discussed in Chap. 4 use a variety of strategies to filter out uninteresting predicates quickly before applying more computationally intensive techniques.

In our running example of comparing x and y, notice that the fundamental predicates logically partition the space of all possibilities, and that summing any two fundamental predicate counters yields an inferred predicate counter for the disjunction. All instrumentation schemes we use have this partition property, which lets us infer one additional piece of information. Summing all of the fundamental predicate counters at a site gives the number of times that the site itself was observed, without regard to any specific predicate at that site. In our running example, we know that $25 + 3 + 1$ observations we made at the site that compares x and y on line 319 of `utils.c`. The site may have been reached many more times than that, but there were exactly 29 times when the site was reached and an observation was made.

2.2.2 Counter-Based Instrumentation Schemes

Within the general approach of predicates and counters, we have many choices as to what predicates are worth counting. Our current implementation offers several instrumentation schemes that have proved useful for isolating a variety of bugs in C programs:

branches

Control flow behavior may reveal places where the program made a fateful decision. The branches scheme considers each control flow decision to be potentially interesting. Each `if` statement induces two fundamental predicates. The first fundamental predicate asserts that the branch is false, while the second fundamental predicate asserts that the branch is true. We treat these two predicates as a single instrumentation site: when the branch is reached, if a sample is due, then exactly one of the two fundamental predicates' counters will be incremented. There are no inferred predicates for this scheme, but we can sum the two predicates at any site to determine how often the site itself was observed.

The branches scheme also counts behavior at many two-way branches that are implicit in C code. The branch governing each while or for loop is instrumented, as is the branch implied by the logical (&&, ||) and conditional (?:) operators. switch statements create multi-way branches; these would require more than two counters per site and are not tracked by the current implementation.

float-kinds

Unusual floating point values may arise during a calculation, propagate from one expression to the next, and only later cause failure. The float-kinds scheme attempts to detect earlier precursors to delayed failures of this kind. We introduce one float-kinds instrumentation site at each assignment to a floating point variable, or at each call to a function that returns a floating point value. Each site tracks the following nine fundamental predicates:

1. returned value is negative infinity $(-\infty)$
2. returned value is negative and normal
3. returned value is negative and denormalized (very close to zero)
4. returned value is negative zero (-0)
5. returned value is not a number (NaN)
6. returned value is positive zero $(+0)$
7. returned value is positive and denormalized (very close to zero)
8. returned value is positive and normal
9. returned value is positive infinity $(+\infty)$

Separately counting every possible floating point value is impractical. This nine-way partition of the set of values is based on numeric classes from the IEEE 754 floating point standard [34]. It captures important sign distinctions and unusual values while requiring only a small number of predicates and predicate counters.

function-entries

Simple function coverage information may reveal which parts of a program are implicated in failures. The function-entries scheme induces one instrumentation site at the entry to each function. This site has one fundamental predicate which is always true. The associated counter, then, is merely a sampled count of the number of times the containing function is called.

g-object-unref

The GLib Object System (*GObject*) provides an object oriented programming framework for C [23]. It serves as the basis for several higher-level toolkits, such as Pango,

GTK+, and GNOME, that are widely used in Linux and Open Source software. GObject manages memory using reference counting, and expects C programmers to manage these reference counts explicitly. We expect that mismanaged reference counts are a common source of hard-to-find heap corruption errors.

The g_object_unref function decrements a GObject instance's reference count. The g-object-unref scheme instruments each such call, inducing one instrumentation site with four fundamental predicates on the state of the object just *before* the decrement:

1. zero references: the instance is already being reclaimed
2. one reference: the instance will be reclaimed within the g_object_unref call that follows
3. more than one reference: the instance is not about to be reclaimed
4. invalid: the argument is not a valid GObject instance

The first and last cases clearly indicate that an error has already happened. The second and third cases, which represent nearly all behavior in practice, may or may not reveal a bug depending on other program behavior. Note that the four fundamental predicates partition the space of all possibilities, with exactly one being incremented per sample. Thus, as in the case of the branches scheme, the sum of all counters at one site gives the approximate (sampled) coverage at that site. We could add inferred predicates corresponding to the disjunctions of the four fundamental predicates, but this has not seemed useful to date.

returns

Function return values can be interesting when used to report the success or failure of various operations. This use is particularly common in C, which lacks exception handling. As for the float-kinds scheme, counting all possible return values is impractical, so the returns instrumentation scheme induces just three fundamental predicates at each function call:

1. returned value is negative
2. returned value is zero
3. returned value is positive

As before, each sample increments exactly one fundamental predicate counter, so the sum of all three of a site's fundamental predicate counters gives approximate coverage at that site. We augment the three fundamental predicates with three inferred predicates whose counts are derived by summing of two of the fundamental predicate counts:

1. returned value is non-negative
2. returned value is non-zero
3. returned value is non-positive

The standard C library makes extensive use of return values as success/failure indicators, and it is often the sign of the returned value that distinguishes success from failure. POSIX follows the same model, as do many programmers. Even within one library there is little consistency as to exactly which sign indicates what. For example, open returns negative values for errors while fopen returns zero (NULL). "Unchecked return values" are a common class of programming error; the returns scheme checks all return values, even those that were ignored by the original program.

This scheme only instruments calls to functions returning characters, integers, and pointers. Pointers are treated as having an unsigned integer type and therefore will only ever be zero (NULL) or positive (non-NULL). Functions that return other types, such as floating point numbers or aggregates, are not instrumented, as these are rarely used to report errors. void-returning functions are not instrumented.

scalar-pairs

Variables within a program often have important relationships with each other or with program constants. Work on the Daikon project has shown that it is useful to identify implicit, often simple invariants as an aide to program evolution [19]. When hunting for bugs, it may be useful to identify near-invariants that are only violated when the program fails.

The scalar-pairs scheme examines possible invariants from a restricted, lightweight subset of the much larger family considered by Daikon. At each assignment to a variable x, identify all other same-typed local or global variables $y_1, y_2, \ldots, y_n$ that are currently in scope. Each pair of variables (x, y_i) induces an instrumentation site that compares the new value of x with the existing value of y_i using three fundamental predicates:

1. $x < y_i$
2. $x = y_i$
3. $x > y_i$

One sample at one site increments one counter for one of these three fundamental predicates. As in the returns scheme, we can sum all three counters for coverage information or sum any two to derive counts for three inferred predicates:

1. $x \geq y_i$
2. $x \neq y_i$
3. $x \leq y_i$

The scalar-pairs scheme only instruments assignments to character-, integer-, or pointer-typed variables. Assignments of aggregates, floating point, and other types are ignored.[1] In its basic form, only assignments to simple named variables are instrumented. Developers who want more detailed instrumentation may also enable

---

[1] The name "scalar-pairs" is therefore a misnomer. The C99 standard considers floating point types to be scalar [36], but we do not currently instrument floating point assignments using this scheme.

instrumenting of assignments across pointers, into structure and union fields, and into indexed arrays. Developers may also allow comparison to constants, in which case x will be compared with every constant expression seen in the program. This list includes, for example, enumeration constants, the element counts of fixed-size arrays, and many other potentially important "magic numbers."

Note that the list of same-typed in-scope variables always includes x itself. In this case, the site is comparing the new value of x on the left side of the comparison to the old value of x on the right side of the comparison. This new-versus-old comparison can be useful to detect bugs due to a failure to monotonically increase or decrease some variable. The value 0 is always included for comparison as well, even if comparison with all program constants is not enabled.

2.2.3 Additional Instrumentation Schemes

In addition to the schemes described above, the current implementation offers several schemes that do not report results as fundamental predicate counters.

ccured

CCured is a source-to-source translator that prevents memory safety violations in C programs [47]. It attempts to prove memory accesses safe at compile time; the remainder are checked at runtime using a variety of assertions. Our ccured instrumentation scheme treats each CCured runtime assertion as a sampled instrumentation site. Thus, the program is no longer guaranteed to detect and block all memory safety violations. Instead it simply has a random chance of detecting each such error. This scheme may be thought of as one example of a more generic instrumentation scheme that randomly samples programmer assertions. In that sense, CCured is simply a source of unusually assertion-dense programs.

bounds

Some bugs are associated with unusually small or large values, such as an out-of-bounds array index or a negative number where only positive values were expected. The bounds scheme induces an instrumentation site at each character-, integer-, or pointer-typed assignment. The site records a pair of values: the minimum and maximum value ever observed at that assignment. Calls to character-, integer-, and pointer-returning functions are instrumented as well, with each site recording the minimum and maximum value ever returned from the associated call.

Unlike the counter-based schemes described earlier, it is not meaningful to add the minimum and maximum values at a site. One can, however, check whether a given site was ever sampled. The minimum value tracker is initialized to the maximum value representable in the given type, while the maximum value tracker is initialized to the minimum representable value.

time stamps

While the case studies in Chap. 4 show that one can go a long way ignoring ordering, we expect there are interesting bugs that require ordering information. The instrumentor implementation currently provides a limited facility for associating time stamps with sampled instrumentation sites. This feature does not constitute an instrumentation scheme in its own right, but rather offers additional information that the developer can choose to overlay on top of any selected schemes.

Time stamping comes in two forms: first-sample and last-sample. In first-sample time stamping, each instrumentation site from any scheme has an additional piece of information associated with it: the time of the first sample actually taken at that site. "Time" here is virtual. We maintain a global "clock" that starts at zero and ticks forward by one each time any instrumentation site is sampled. Thus first-sample time stamping yields a record of the relative orders in which sites were first sampled.

Last-sample time stamping also gives each site a snapshot of the global clock value at the moment a sample is taken. Here we update that snapshot on every sample of a site rather than only the first. Thus last-sample time stamping yields a record of the relative orders in which sites were last sampled leading up to program termination.

Clearly these time stamps form an incomplete record of program behavior. One cannot distinguish multiple samples at one site. With sparse sampling, most sites are reached but not sampled, so even the site with first-sample time stamp of "1" is probably not the first site actually reached during execution. However, these time stamps do provide at least some information. They may be particularly useful in isolating bugs due to improper ordering of initialization or finalization logic; code handling these tasks typically runs just once per execution, so multiple sample ambiguity is less of a problem.

One possible approach to using time stamps is to infer predicates "a first sampled before b" and "a last sampled before b" on all pairs of sites (a, b). (One might also write these more formally as predicates over program traces in linear temporal logic.) Existing algorithms, described in Chap. 4, may be applied to these predicates to discover which ones are predictive of failure. However, it is important to note that multi-event predicates rapidly become hard to observe: a base sampling rate of $1/100$ implies only a $1/10,000$ chance of observing any pair of independent events. It may be difficult to obtain enough time stamp data to draw statistically significant conclusions. To date, we have not experimented much with the time stamping facility, and so its usefulness in practice remains unknown.

2.3 Performance and Optimizations

For ubiquitous monitoring to be practical, it must be lightweight. Users have better things to do then wait around while an application ploddingly debugs itself. In this section we assess the performance impact of both unconditional and sampled instrumentation. We consider the basic strategy described above as well as a number of optimizations specially tuned to code produced by the sampling transformation.

Table 2.1. Instrumentation overhead in typical configuration (continues on next page)

Scheme	Benchmark	Overhead For Sampling Rate				
		Always	$1/10$	$1/100$	$1/1,000$	$1/10,000$
branches	bh	46%	210%	32%	16%	13%
	bisort	50%	159%	19%	0%	0%
	compress	134%	463%	80%	38%	31%
	em3d	61%	225%	42%	23%	21%
	health	18%	40%	4%	1%	0%
	ijpeg	113%	406%	62%	24%	20%
	mst	17%	42%	11%	7%	7%
	perimeter	84%	551%	127%	83%	77%
	power	8%	136%	16%	2%	-2%
	treeadd	15%	44%	8%	4%	4%
	tsp	106%	161%	19%	5%	3%
	vortex	160%	585%	100%	47%	33%
returns	bh	9%	30%	13%	11%	12%
	bisort	6%	49%	6%	0%	0%
	compress	5%	39%	9%	6%	4%
	em3d	1%	2%	1%	-1%	-1%
	health	2%	-1%	-5%	-4%	-5%
	ijpeg	5%	40%	7%	5%	3%
	mst	23%	25%	7%	5%	5%
	perimeter	61%	236%	48%	27%	24%
	power	1%	0%	0%	0%	0%
	treeadd	27%	49%	8%	5%	5%
	tsp	9%	3%	0%	-1%	0%
	vortex	36%	116%	30%	23%	19%

We have measured the performance of instrumented code using a collection of twelve CPU-intensive benchmarks selected from the SPEC CPU95 [57] and Olden [11] suites. Our basis for comparison is the same code compiled with no instrumentation whatsoever. We consider a range of sampling rates, and also a special "always" configuration in which instrumentation is added but the sampling transformation is not applied. This configuration lets us explore whether the speed boost from having a fast path is enough to compensate for the overhead of sampling itself, such as region checks and countdown management.

Table 2.1 gives the overhead for each benchmark at each sampling rate. Overhead here is measured as increase in wall clock run time as compared with instrumentation-free code. We present results for three of the instrumentation schemes described earlier: branches, returns, and scalar-pairs. The scalar-pairs scheme is used here with comparison to variables and 0 only, not to other program constants. A fourth "all of above" pseudo-scheme simultaneously uses branches, returns, and scalar-pairs instrumentation in a single binary. All measurements were taken on one CPU of a

Table 2.1. Instrumentation overhead in typical configuration (continued)

		Overhead For Sampling Rate				
Scheme	Benchmark	Always	$\frac{1}{10}$	$\frac{1}{100}$	$\frac{1}{1,000}$	$\frac{1}{10,000}$
scalar-pairs	bh	533%	5,043%	720%	120%	22%
	bisort	471%	2,112%	274%	69%	44%
	compress	1,899%	8,764%	1,113%	175%	72%
	em3d	164%	862%	101%	21%	12%
	health	34%	173%	16%	2%	2%
	ijpeg	1,322%	6,171%	799%	135%	41%
	mst	74%	397%	52%	13%	8%
	perimeter	105%	814%	110%	30%	22%
	power	-2%	239%	29%	11%	8%
	treeadd	60%	412%	51%	9%	4%
	tsp	42%	191%	26%	3%	1%
	vortex	616%	3,987%	555%	105%	45%
all of above	bh	576%	5,205%	731%	126%	28%
	bisort	570%	2,309%	301%	69%	44%
	compress	2,049%	9,075%	1,202%	191%	74%
	em3d	226%	1,118%	136%	35%	25%
	health	41%	230%	22%	5%	1%
	ijpeg	1,422%	6,627%	869%	149%	46%
	mst	86%	452%	62%	15%	10%
	perimeter	209%	1,565%	246%	99%	76%
	power	23%	406%	55%	19%	16%
	treeadd	69%	524%	62%	12%	7%
	tsp	140%	359%	51%	9%	4%
	vortex	804%	4,708%	679%	130%	60%

four-way 2.8 GHz Intel Xeon SMP with 3.7 GB RAM. The host is running Fedora Core 2 with Linux kernel version 2.6.8. The C runtime library is `glibc` version 2.3.3, vendor-supplied without instrumentation. All benchmarks were compiled using GCC version 3.4.3 with "-O3" and no other special optimization flags. Our instrumentor was used in its typical configuration. This configuration includes a number of default optimizations that we discuss at greater length below. Each percentage in the table represents an average across five runs with five distinct random seeds. Repeated runs in the same environment, or changing only the seed, show negligible variation.

First considering just the "Always" column, observe that overheads vary tremendously between benchmarks and instrumentation schemes. If the purpose of sampling is to reduce overhead, we have starting overheads ranging from 2,049% (a major slowdown when all three schemes are simultaneously applied to the compress benchmark) to -2% (a slight speedup when scalar-pairs instrumentation is applied to the power benchmark). Instrumentation schemes vary in their aggressiveness, with some adding far more sites than others. But overhead can vary widely even within a single scheme: scalar-pairs with unconditional ("always") instrumentation causes

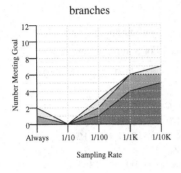

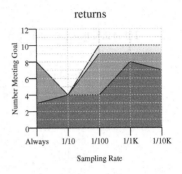

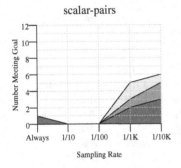

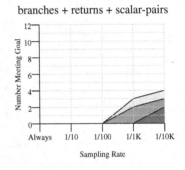

Fig. 2.2. Benchmarks meeting performance goals in typical configuration: overhead $\leq 5\%$
(■), overhead $\leq 10\%$ (▨), and overhead $\leq 15\%$ (▢)

the compress benchmark to run 1,899% slower but causes the power benchmark to run 2% faster. This variation shows that deployment of any of these instrumentation schemes cannot be a mindless, purely mechanical process. One must consider the specific properties of the code in question, identify critical bottlenecks, and intelligently weigh the desire to collect data against the need to maintain acceptable performance. What constitutes "acceptable" is inherently domain specific: a numerically intensive simulation has different requirements from a web browser or a database transaction server. The particular example of power running 2% faster with unconditional scalar-pairs instrumentation also highlights the fact that any code perturbation can randomly shift performance by a few percentage points due to measurement noise, cache alignment changes, and other hard-to-control-for factors.

Figure 2.2 presents an alternate view of the same data, summarized to allow easier identification of trends. We choose 5%, 10%, and 15% as somewhat arbitrary overhead goals, and count how many of the twelve benchmarks meet each of those goals. For example, suppose we are interested in the returns instrumentation scheme with $1/100$ sampling. Then the upper-right ("returns") graph shows that four benchmarks have 5% overhead or less; five benchmarks have between 5% and 10% overhead; one benchmark has between 10% and 15% overhead; and the remaining two benchmarks have more than 15% overhead.

These graphs clearly show that some schemes are more lightweight than others. The returns scheme is especially cheap, with most benchmarks showing low overhead even without sampling. For some applications, one might reasonably decide to deploy this scheme in "always" mode, collecting complete data without sampling. The scalar-pairs scheme is the most costly, due to two factors. First, scalar-pairs adds far more individual instrumentation sites than any other scheme. This means a larger memory footprint, more observations, more countdown management, and more time spent on the slow path. Second, scalar-pairs instrumentation sites include many comparisons between pairs of local variables. This artificially enlarges the live ranges of local variables, increasing register pressure and making register allocation substantially less effective.

In each scheme, a pronounced dip at $1/10$ reveals that this rate is too dense to be beneficial. At such a high sampling rate, not enough time is spent in the fast path to overcome the overhead of the sampling infrastructure. Thus $1/10$ sampling performs worse than unconditional instrumentation. Performance improves across the board as we reduce the rate to $1/100$. This rate is roughly the break even point at which sampling and always-on instrumentation have comparable overhead. Of course, given a choice between only these two, one would opt for "always" as it provides more complete data. However, we can buy back even more performance by further reducing the sampling rate. $1/1,000$ consistently outperforms unconditional instrumentation. Most schemes do continue to improve at $1/10,000$, suggesting that their performance ceilings reside at yet sparser sampling rates. Referring back to Table 2.1, improvements from $1/1,000$ to $1/10,000$ are largest for exactly those benchmarks that perform the worst, such as bh, compress, and vortex. Sparser random sampling increases the effective noise level of the sampled data relative to ideal, complete data. So even if some application continues speed up at, say, $1/10^9$ sampling, that may not be practical relative to the size of that application's user base and the time one is willing to wait in order to find bugs. Section 2.5 considers these trade-offs in greater detail.

The subsections that follow describe and evaluate several specific optimizations that have been implemented or proposed. Overall, we find that most of the optimizations implemented to date have no significant effect on performance. With few exceptions, the performance profile depicted in Fig. 2.2 remains largely unchanged. However, it is important to keep in mind that these are CPU-intensive benchmarks. One would expect to see worse performance here than on more realistic, complete applications. Performance has not been an issue, at least so far, in the applications we have studied and deployed. One would also expect that less invasive instrumentation strategies (e.g. returns) perform better than more invasive ones (e.g. scalar-pairs), and they do. The surprise is that performance remains slower than we would like on some benchmarks even with multiple optimizations and with sampling rates very close to zero. This suggests the presence of tight inner loops with little chance to amortize the cost of deciding between the fast and slow paths. In such situations, loop unrolling may offer a way to make acyclic regions larger and amortization more effective. We

branches

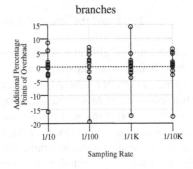

returns

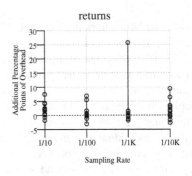

scalar-pairs

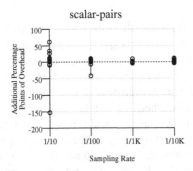

branches + returns + scalar-pairs

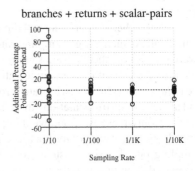

Fig. 2.3. Change in overhead without static branch prediction. Positive numbers indicate larger overhead relative to typical configuration.

can also simply avoid instrumenting selected performance critical sections of code. Subsection 2.3.7 considers this selective exclusion technique in greater detail.

2.3.1 Static Branch Prediction

As discussed in Sect. 2.1.1, each acyclic region of a transformed control flow graph chooses between fast and slow variants depending on the current next sample count-down and the threshold weight of that region. When sampling is sparse, this threshold check will usually branch into the fast path. This fact creates a good opportunity for static branch prediction. We pass a hint to the native C compiler using __builtin_expect, a non-standard GCC extension.

In theory, this static branch prediction helps GCC's optimizer make better code generation and layout decisions. In practice, the effects are small. Table 2.1 and Fig. 2.2 included static branch prediction. Figure 2.3 shows how overheads grow or shrink when static branch prediction hints are omitted.

In these graphs, each circle represents a single benchmark at a single sampling rate. Positive numbers represent increases in overhead relative to the typical instrumentor configuration; negative numbers represent reductions in overhead. To take an extreme example, Table 2.1 reports that with scalar-pairs instrumentation and $1/10$ sampling, the compress benchmark exhibits 8,764% overhead in the typical instrumentor configuration. If static branch prediction hints are omitted, this overhead shrinks to 8,611, for a net overhead reduction of 153 percentage points. The lower left ("scalar-pairs") graph shows one circle at -153 for sampling rate $1/10$ representing this reduction in overhead for one benchmark.

Based on this information, static branch prediction hints at the tops of acyclic regions are not a clear benefit. Most overheads change by only a few percentage points, and as many benchmarks speed up as slow down. Measurement noise and random effects such as cache alignment likely account for most of these small perturbations. The perimeter benchmark, however, is an interesting counterexample. When run with branches instrumentation, perimeter consistently shows between 15 and 20 percentage points lower overhead when static branch prediction hints are disabled. This is visible as four circles running along the bottom edge of the top left ("branches") graph. The size of this change is fairly consistent even though the actual overhead varies from 551% to 77% depending on the sampling rate. It is unclear why this particular benchmark so consistently improves without static branch prediction hints. We suspect that the hints may be causing GCC to make heuristic code layout decisions that are helpful for most code but that happen to be harmful for the perimeter benchmark.

One can artificially construct a program with very large acyclic regions. In such a program, acyclic region threshold weights are high and therefore the slow path is often used. Static branch prediction hints in such a program would be more often wrong than right, creating additional overhead unless hints are disabled. However, any such large-region effect would be especially pronounced at dense sampling rates, and we see no such trend in the data shown in Fig. 2.3. Therefore, overly large acyclic regions do not appear to be a problem for these benchmarks.

2.3.2 Weightless Functions

Subsection 2.1.3 conservatively assumed that any function call might change the next sample countdown arbitrarily. Therefore, a new threshold check must appear immediately after each function call. This treatment is appropriate if, e.g., the caller and callee are being compiled separately.

However, if the callee is known and available for examination while compiling the caller, a simple interprocedural analysis can be used to refine this conservative assumption. Define a *weightless function* as one with following properties:

- The function contains no instrumentation sites.
- The function only calls other weightless functions.

The set of weightless functions can be computed via a standard fixpoint algorithm, requiring no more iterations than the depth of the longest non-recursive call chain.

For purposes of identifying acyclic regions and introducing threshold checks, calls to weightless functions are invisible. Acyclic regions can extend below such

branches

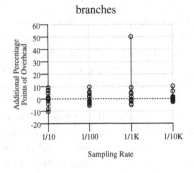

returns

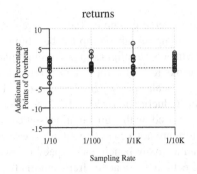

scalar-pairs

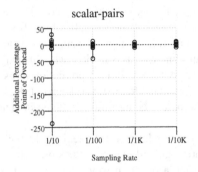

branches + returns + scalar-pairs

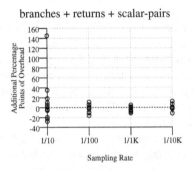

Fig. 2.4. Change in overhead without weightless function optimization. Positive numbers indicate larger overhead relative to typical configuration.

calls, and no additional threshold check is required after such a call returns. A further benefit is that the bodies of weightless functions may be compiled with no modifications. They have no threshold checks, no instrumented code, and therefore require no cloning or transformation of any kind.

The current instrumentor implementation performs weightless function analysis for direct, statically bound calls within a single compilation unit. Dynamically bound calls across function pointers are conservatively assumed to be non-weightless ("weighty") pending integration of a points-to analysis. Called functions in separate compilation units are also assumed to be weighty unless explicitly declared otherwise via a special preprocessor pragma. As a special case, all functions in the standard C runtime libraries (libc and libm) are assumed weightless with the exception of:

- bsearch and qsort, which may call weighty comparison predicates,
- setjmp, longjmp, and a few related functions, which perform interprocedural control transfer.

Table 2.1 and Fig. 2.2 included optimization of calls to weightless functions. Figure 2.3 shows how overheads grow or shrink when this optimization is disabled by assuming that all functions are weighty. Again, positive numbers represent larger overheads without this optimization. Negative numbers represent smaller overheads without this optimization. Overall we find no consistent benefit or harm. Special treatment of calls to weightless functions does not have an appreciable, reliable effect on performance.

2.3.3 Empty and Singleton Regions

Two special cases arise after computing the threshold weights of acyclic regions. A region may contain no instrumentation sites, giving it threshold weight zero. The sampling transformation disregards any such regions. They require no threshold check and no slow/fast code cloning. In effect, we generate only the fast path; the slow path would be dead code and therefore is omitted. If a loop contains no instrumentation sites, then the instrumentor need not even treat the loop as a cycle. An "acyclic" region may actually include an arbitrary number of instrumentation-free loops.

The second special case concerns singleton regions: those with threshold weight one. Any path through such a region crosses at most one instrumentation site. Crossing one instrumentation site entails decrement and check of the next sample countdown. However, even the fast path would have one check (the top-of-region threshold check) and one decrement (where the instrumentation site would otherwise appear). Therefore, the fast path for singleton regions is no faster than the slow path. Instead of generating both, we omit the fast path, omit the top-of-region threshold check, and only generate code for the slow path. Note that this optimization applies to any region with threshold weight one, even if multiple sites appear within the region. A region consisting of a branch with one site on each arm is still a singleton region, as any path through that region crosses at most one site.

Table 2.1 and Fig. 2.2 included empty and singleton region specialization. Figure 2.3 shows how overheads grow or shrink when this optimization is disabled and empty and singleton regions are cloned into fast and slow paths like all other regions. Positive numbers indicate that disabling region specialization makes code slower. In the branches and returns schemes we see a general trend toward larger overheads without this optimization. Inversely, special treatment of empty and singleton regions shrinks overhead by roughly three to five percentage points with these schemes. The effect, while small, is consistent across multiple benchmarks and sampling rates and therefore appears to be genuine.

The scalar-pairs scheme adds a very large amount of instrumentation. Almost any fragment of realistic code will induce multiple instrumentation sites, so empty and singleton regions are rare when the scalar-pairs scheme is in use. This is visible as a lack of a clear positive or negative trend in the lower left ("scalar-pairs") and lower right ("branches + returns + scalar-pairs") graphs of Fig. 2.3. The optimization does no harm in these cases; it is merely inapplicable.

2.3.4 Local Countdown Caching

Careful examination of the assembly code produced for instrumented applications reveals that having the next-site countdown in a global variable can be expensive.

branches

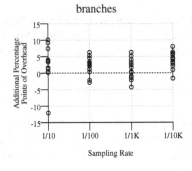

returns

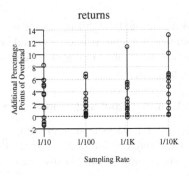

scalar-pairs

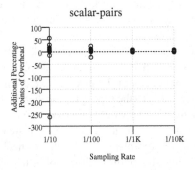

branches + returns + scalar-pairs

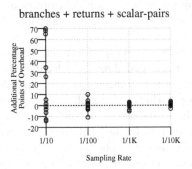

Fig. 2.5. Change in overhead without region specialization. Positive numbers indicate larger overhead relative to typical configuration.

Our native C compiler, GCC, treats the many "--countdown" decrements along the fast path quite poorly. It will not, for example, coalesce a sequence of five such decrements into a single "countdown -= 5" adjustment. This lack of optimization apparently stems from conservative assumptions about aliasing of global variables.

Efficient countdown management requires that the native C compiler take greater liberties when optimizing these decrements. We assist the native compiler by caching the countdown in a local variable within each function:

1. At function entry, *import* the current global countdown into a local variable.
2. Use this locally cached countdown for all decrements, threshold checks, and sampling decisions.
3. Just before function exit, *export* the locally cached countdown back out to the global.

To maintain agreement across all functions, we must also export just before each function call and import again after each call returns. Again, though, calls to weightless functions may simply be ignored, as they do not change or even inspect the countdown. Similarly, the bodies of weightless functions need not import and export at entry and exit, since they always leave the countdown unchanged. With

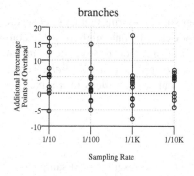

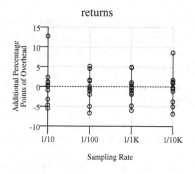

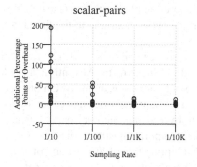

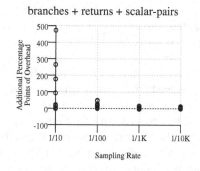

Fig. 2.6. Change in overhead without local next sample countdown cache. Positive numbers indicate larger overhead relative to typical configuration.

this change, the conventional native C compiler can coalesce decrements, store the cached countdown in a register, and perform other standard optimizations.

Table 2.1 and Fig. 2.2 cached the next sample countdown in local variables. Figure 2.3 shows how overheads grow or shrink when a local variable cache is not used, and the next sample countdown is accessed directly as a global variable. Positive numbers indicate that disabling countdown caching makes code slower.

In the lower left and lower right graphs, where the scalar-pairs scheme is active, we find large increases in overhead without the local countdown cache. Because scalar-pairs adds so many instrumentation sites, the next sample countdown is accessed very frequently. Even straight line code may cross multiple instrumentation sites, so decrement coalescing is important here too. The beneficial effect of using a local cache is pronounced at dense sampling rates, such as 1/10 and 1/100, but extends to sparser rates as well.

The benefits of this optimization come at a cost: extra import operations are required to keep the local and global countdowns consistent across function calls. When calls to weighty functions are common, and acyclic regions small, this additional bookkeeping may overwhelm the benefits of using the local cache. The branches and returns schemes show no clear benefit to local countdown caching, possibly due to these import/export costs. If further study confirms that these costs are a problem, alternate approaches are possible. For example, one might pass the count-down from caller to callee as an additional function argument or store the countdown in a dedicated global register. Care must be taken to apply such a coordinated change in a way that does not break non-instrumented callers or callees in a mixed-code environment.

2.3.5 Random Countdown Generation

Subsection 2.1.1 enumerated the operations required to reset the next sample count-down after each measurement. Amortization helps share the cost of these operations. For an additional performance boost, one might instead generate a bank of random countdowns offline, before starting the instrumented application. An instrumented application consumes them from first to last, and may wrap around to the first again if too few were provided.

Our implementation supports this alternate strategy. Banks of 1,021 random countdowns may be generated offline and stored in binary form. At runtime a bank is mapped into memory using mmap and accessed efficiently as an array. On our reference platform, the Intel IA-32 (a.k.a. $x86$), one countdown occupies four bytes, so 1,021 countdowns fit within a single four kilobyte virtual memory page. Furthermore, 1,021 is prime, reducing the chance of bad temporal aliasing with any periodic behavior within the application. With a typical sampling rate of $1/100$, a bank of 1,021 random countdowns covers an average of 102,100 site crossings before repeating.

An even faster approach eschews randomization entirely, and always resets the next sample countdown to a fixed value, such as 100 for a sampling rate of $1/100$. As discussed in Sect. 2.1.1, this approach runs a high risk of creating temporal aliasing with periodic program behaviors. The data collected may no longer be a truly fair, representative sample of complete program behavior. However, fixed-period sampling may be a useful strategy to consider when performance is so important as to trump strict statistical correctness. Extremely common, repeating program behaviors will still be visible, which made periodic sampling reasonable for Arnold and Ryder to use when hunting performance bottlenecks [2]. However, rare bugs, or bugs caused by rare behaviors, risk being systematically lost due to temporal aliasing.

Table 2.1 and Fig. 2.2 used online generation of random countdowns as needed. Figure 2.7 shows how overheads grow or shrink when countdowns are generated offline. Figure 2.8 shows how overheads grow or shrink when countdowns are not random at all, but instead use a fixed reset value of d for sampling rate $1/d$. High sampling rates consume random countdowns more rapidly, and these results show that random countdown generation is indeed a major source of overhead when sampling is dense. The scalar-pairs scheme magnifies this same effect: speeding up countdown generation is critical when using this instrumentation-intensive scheme at high sampling rates.

For sparse sampling rates, a single countdown lasts longer and therefore the cost of generating the next countdown is less significant. No consistent performance boost is seen at $1/1,000$ and $1/10,000$ for either offline or fixed countdowns. This result suggests

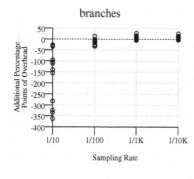

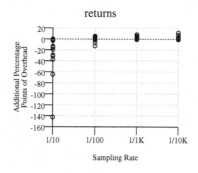

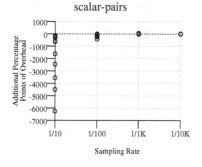

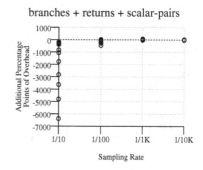

Fig. 2.7. Change in overhead with offline random countdown generation. Positive numbers indicate larger overhead relative to typical configuration.

that the cost of true statistical fairness is not excessive in cases such as bug hunting, where rare events may carry great significance.

2.3.6 Path Balancing

When the fast path consists of simple, straight-line code, the C compiler may be able to coalesce multiple countdown decrements into a single larger adjustment. For example, GCC performs this optimization provided that the countdown is cached in a local variable per Sect. 2.3.4. However, decrement coalescing cannot extend across branches, because the multiple forward paths may contain different numbers of instrumentation sites and therefore require different net adjustments to the countdown.

Path balancing generalizes decrement coalescing to arbitrary acyclic regions. The key is to ensure that all forward paths through an acyclic region cross the same number of instrumentation sites. Imbalances occur at branches. When a control flow graph node has multiple successor paths with different weights, extra "dummy" sites are added to the start of those successor paths that have fewer "real" sites than their siblings, thereby creating balance. When all branches in a region are balanced, the entire region is balanced as well.

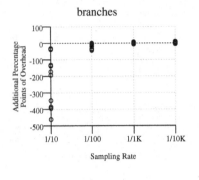

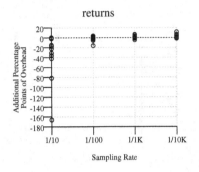

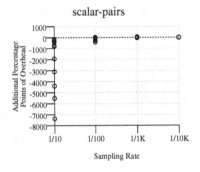

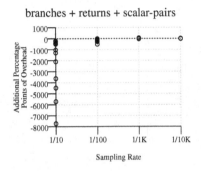

Fig. 2.8. Change in overhead with fixed, non-random countdown. Positive numbers indicate larger overhead relative to typical configuration.

Figure 2.9a gives an example of an acyclic region before balancing. Nodes with instrumentation sites have dotted outlines. Notes are lettered for ease of reference, and the number in each node gives the maximum weight of all paths forward from that node. The entire region has threshold weight 2 but individual paths cross 0 (*abe*), 1 (*adh*), or 2 (*abcfg*, *abcfh*) sites. Branch nodes *a*, *b*, and *f* may require balancing. Branch *a* does have imbalanced successors: one dummy site must be added on the *ad* edge. Branch *b* is also imbalanced: two dummy sites must be added on the *be* edge. Branch *f* is already balanced: both successors already have matching weights.

Figure 2.9b shows the same acyclic region after balancing. Three unlettered dummy sites have been added. The threshold weight for the entire region (2) is now the exact number of sites crossed on each of the four paths through the region starting from entry node *a*.

Balancing is not an optimization in and of itself. Rather, it actually adds instrumentation in the form of dummy sites. However, once a site is balanced, we can optimize the code as follows. Just before the first node of the fast path, decrement the next sample countdown by the threshold weight of the entire region (for example, "countdown -= 2" just before node *a* in Fig. 2.9b). This increment accounts for exactly the number of unary decrements that would have occurred in this region.

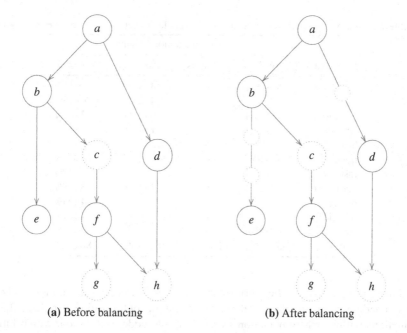

(a) Before balancing   (b) After balancing

Fig. 2.9. Example of path balancing

Elsewhere in the fast path, wherever a real or dummy instrumentation site would have appeared, do nothing. The decrements have already been accounted for and there is no other work to do.

The slow path must decrement and check the countdown at each instrumentation site as before, because on the slow path we do need to know exactly when a site should be sampled. Furthermore, even dummy sites must decrement the countdown and reset it if it reaches zero. This requirement ensures that both the fast and slow paths behave the same with respect to counting down to the next sample, at the expense of making the slow path even slower. Also, adding dummy instrumentation sites means that the countdown will need to be reset more often, so a slow random number generator will be more of a liability here.

In total, path balancing makes the fast path faster and the slow path slower. The path balancing algorithm has not yet been implemented. Evaluating its net effect on performance is left as future work.

2.3.7 Statically Selective Sampling

It is not necessary to put all instrumentation into a single executable; one can easily create multiple executables where each contains a subset of the complete instrumentation. Partitioning instrumentation by site, by module, by function, or by object file are all reasonable strategies. Any individual executable contains less instrumentation

Table 2.2. Number and percentage of functions excluded to achieve 15% performance goals

Benchmark	Instrumentation Scheme			
	branches	returns	scalar-pairs	all of above
bh	1 (2%)	-	3 (7%)	5 (12%)
bisort	-	-	4 (25%)	4 (25%)
compress	3 (13%)	-	6 (26%)	7 (30%)
em3d	1 (7%)	-	1 (7%)	2 (13%)
health	-	-	-	-
ijpeg	4 (1%)	-	10 (2%)	11 (2%)
mst	2 (14%)	-	-	1 (7%)
perimeter	3 (38%)	1 (13%)	1 (13%)	3 (38%)
power	-	-	-	4 (24%)
treeadd	-	-	-	1 (11%)
tsp	1 (8%)	-	-	-
vortex	35 (4%)	12 (1%)	53 (6%)	88 (10%)

and therefore incurs a smaller performance penalty. Fewer sites mean more weight-less functions, and therefore better interprocedural optimization per Sect. 2.3.2. Functions without instrumentation sites require no code duplication, which limits executable growth. Known trusted code can be exempted from instrumentation, or especially suspect code can be "farmed out" to a larger proportion of users for more intensive study. Given a suitable dynamic instrumentation infrastructure, sites can be added or removed over time as debugging needs and intermediate results warrant.

We have experimented with benchmarks in which only a single function is instrumented at a time, using the CCured instrumentation scheme. Whereas fully instrumented executables range from 13%-149% larger than their non-sampling counterparts, average code growth for single-function instrumented executables is just 12% for the small Olden benchmarks and 6% for the larger SPEC CPU95 applications. Performance is uniformly good: at $1/1,000$ sampling, 94% of site-containing functions incur less than 5% slowdown versus instrumentation-free code, while even the worst single function has less than a 12% penalty.

Instead of instrumenting one function at a time, we might start with a fully instrumented application and then selectively exclude high-traffic functions from instrumentation. We can exclude functions in this manner, one at a time, until performance reaches desired levels on some test suite believed to be representative of real world usage patterns. The set of high-traffic functions can itself be refined over time using coverage information derived from feedback reports as suggested in Sect. 2.2.2. The same process could be applied at a finer-grained level, such as basic blocks or even individual statements or instrumentation sites. Function exclusion is sufficient here to demonstrate the technique.

Figure 2.2 showed that many benchmarks fail to reach a performance goal of 15% maximum overhead when all functions are instrumented. We have iteratively excluded functions in each benchmark, for each instrumentation scheme, until the overhead at $^1/_{1,000}$ sampling was no greater than 15%. Table 2.2 shows how many functions had to be excluded in each case, as an absolute count of functions and as a percentage of all non-library functions in the benchmark. Benchmark and scheme configurations that met the 15% goal with no exclusion at all are listed as "-". In general we find that the absolute number of excluded functions is small in the small benchmarks, although the percentage may appear large. Conversely, the percentage of excluded functions is small in the larger benchmarks, although the absolute count may appear large. These results suggest that for CPU intensive applications it is a reasonable compromise to identify and exclude a small performance-critical kernel to achieve low overheads while retaining the benefits of sampled instrumentation elsewhere in the application.

2.3.8 Optimization Recap

The experiments of this section show that we can instrument and sample code with reasonable performance, although we may have to resort to excluding some performance critical code to achieve that with our current implementation. Two remaining sources of overhead that we have identified are the instrumentation code left on the fast path and suboptimal code due to being forced to rely on the whims of the native compiler's optimizer. Improvements to the instrumentation algorithm, such as path balancing, can solve the first problem. Binary rewriting techniques can address the second, as demonstrated in recent work by Chilimbi et al. (see Sect. 5.2). We have not explored either avenue further to date because the performance of our existing implementation has thus far been more than adequate for our experiments and public deployment. Developing a better understanding of the performance characteristics of sampled instrumentation remains an important area for future work.

2.4 Adaptive Sampling

Our basic instrumentation strategy treats all sites equally. Each site is observed in linear proportion to the number of times it is reached, modulo random sampling. However, not all program behaviors are equally interesting, especially when looking for bugs. One might want more detailed information about newly written code, novice code, complex code, rarely executed code, security-sensitive code, code implementing brittle features, or code that raises a red flag in the developer's mind for any other reason. Nonuniform sampling requires both a policy to decide what is interesting as well as a mechanism for translating that interest into adjusted sampling rates.

We present here two mechanisms for varying the sampling rate across different instrumentation sites followed by some general notes on policy selection.

2.4.1 Nonuniformity Via Multiple Countdowns

We can implement nonuniform sampling using multiple global next sample countdowns instead of just a single countdown. At run time, maintain several countdowns tuned to different average sampling rates, such as $1/1$, $1/100$ and $1/10,000$. (A "random" $1/1$ countdown is always reset to exactly 1, thereby sampling at every opportunity.) Each acyclic region is bound to one of these countdowns, and the threshold weight check and all countdown decrements use the bound countdown. In simple cases, bindings can be static. If the adaptation policy requires post-deployment changes, either binary patching or an extra level of indirection can be used to change each region's binding at program launch time or even dynamically as the program runs.

Multiple countdowns are conceptually straightforward, though they complicate the instrumentation process in practice and therefore have not yet been implemented. It is easy to directly set the sampling rate for any acyclic region. Any desired rate may be used, though implementations might choose to limit the total number of distinct global countdowns. Because countdowns are bound on a per-region basis, all sites within an acyclic region must use the same sampling rate, and a site appearing in multiple regions forces rate matching on all of them. However, acyclic regions need not be maximal. If the rate-matching restriction is found to be problematic at instrumentation time, a large region can be subdivided into smaller ones bound to distinct countdowns.

2.4.2 Nonuniformity Via Non-Unit Site Weights

Throughout Sect. 2.1 we assumed that each site had identical, unit weight. The threshold weight of a region is the largest total weight of sites crossed on any one path through that region. However, we need not restrict ourselves to unit weights. We might select an arbitrary site of interest and assign it weight two. Upon reaching that site, we decrement the next sample countdown twice, and take a sample if either decrement drives the countdown to zero. When computing acyclic region threshold weights, any path crossing this "heavier" site adds a weight of two instead of one. The effect is as though we had two copies of the site in sequence. A site with weight three will be observed even more frequently. In general, if the core, underlying sampling rate is $1/d$, and execution reaches an instrumentation site with weight w, then the probability of making an observation is

$$1 - (1 - 1/d)^w. \tag{2.1}$$

This formula gives the probability of seeing at least one success (equivalently, not seeing w failures) in w trials of a $1/d$ Bernoulli process. Weights must be natural numbers, so a given core rate defines a discrete family of derived sampling rates. For $d = 10$, the available sampling rates include $\{0.1, 0.19, 0.271, 0.3439, \ldots\}$. For $d = 1,000$, the available sampling rates include $\{0.001, 0.001999, 0.002997, 0.003994, \ldots\}$. Sparser core rates yield smaller steps between derived rates. In all cases, the least sampling probability is $1/d$ when $w = 1$, while the sampling probability asymptotically approaches 1 as w increases without bound. (In practice, if the countdown is stored as a 32-bit unsigned integer, then setting w to $2^{32} - 1$ guarantees that every possible sample will be taken.)

This approach offers both benefits and drawbacks compared to using multiple countdowns. Implementation is simpler, and this approach is already available for use in the instrumentor. Weights need not be uniform within an acyclic region. A much larger family of sampling rates is available. On the other hand, one does not have truly arbitrary rates, only those derived from the core sampling rate. The hyperbolic curve defined by Equation 2.1 has some inconvenient properties. Doubling a site's weight does not double its sampling rate. Doubling the core sampling rate does not uniformly double the sampling rates for all sites: the actual rate increase depends on each site's weight. If one wants to maintain certain proportions between the sampling rates of different sites, site weights must be changed with any change to the core rate, and certain proportions may be impossible to achieve exactly. Both schemes allow for adaptive sampling: weights can be patched in at a binary level or else read from an external manifest. One does need to recompute regions' threshold weights, though, based on the weights assigned to their contained sites. This calculation requires some extra bookkeeping that the multiple countdowns scheme avoids.

In principle, these two mechanisms can coexist. One can provide multiple countdowns, with each region bound to one countdown and each site within that region assigned its own weight. This hybrid approach offers maximum flexibility at a price of maximum engineering complexity.

2.4.3 Policy Notes

At present we have only limited experience with different policies for deciding which sites are worth closer attention. We note, however, that nonuniform sampling for bug isolation is especially well matched to a policy based on code coverage. Empirical studies show that rarely executed code exhibits higher defect density than frequently used code [29, 33], an effect that is even more pronounced post-deployment [30]. Denser sampling of rarely executed code, even as high as $1/1$ (complete data), should have a relatively small impact on performance, while sparser sampling of heavily used code will improve performance. Thus nonuniform sampling based on code coverage should provide useful debugging information while simultaneously reducing overhead. Subsection 4.4.1 and Sect. 4.6 define and use one such coverage-guided policy.

2.5 Realistic Sampling Rates

From the benchmarks of Sect. 2.3 and the case studies in Chap. 4, we conclude that realistic deployments will use sampling densities between $1/100$ and $1/1,000$. But how effective is $1/1,000$ sampling at observing rare program behavior? Suppose we are interested in an event occurring once per hundred executions. To achieve 90% confidence of observing this event in at least one run, we need at least

$$\frac{\log{(1 - 0.90)}}{\log{\left(1 - \frac{1}{100} \times \frac{1}{1,000}\right)}} = 230{,}257 \text{ runs.}$$

While 230,257 is a large number of runs, consider that sixty million Office XP licenses were sold in its first year on the market [42]. Assuming that the average licensee runs Microsoft Word twice per week, then this user base produces 230,257 runs every nineteen minutes. Achieving 99% confidence of observing an event that occurs on one in a thousand runs requires 4,605,170 runs, which takes less than seven hours to gather.

For smaller deployments, we must either wait longer for sufficient data or increase the sampling density. As we will see in Sect. 4.2 and Sect. 4.3, at least for restricted classes of bugs we can perform useful analysis with a few thousand executions. Thus, our techniques are likely most suited to applications where it is possible to gather data with at least $1/1,000$ sampling from thousands of executions per day.

3

Practical Considerations

It compiles. Ship it.

−Bart Schaefer, Vice President of Engineering,
Z-Code Software Corporation

We believe that CBI and related research efforts have great potential to make software development more responsive and efficient by giving developers accurate data about how software is actually used in deployment. However, testing this idea requires significant experimentation with real, and preferably large, user communities using real applications. This chapter reports on our experience in preparing for such experiments.

We have selected several large open source applications, listed in Table 3.1, comprising some two million lines of code before instrumentation. We have built instrumented packages using the strategy described in Chap. 2, made these packages available to the public, and are now in the process of collecting feedback reports. We have not yet identified any bugs using these reports: our user base is still too small, and does not provide reports in the quantities needed by our statistical debugging techniques. However, we have demonstrated an end-to-end complete CBI system and feel comfortable in claiming that our approach is technically feasible. While aspects of our system could certainly be improved, at this point all components are good enough to support the deployment of realistic instrumented applications and the collection of feedback reports from a large user community.

Table 3.1. Applications from the public deployment

Application	Lines of Code	Shared Libraries	Plugins	Threads
EVOLUTION	574,224	✓	✓	✓
GAIM	209,639		✓	
THE GIMP	657,156	✓	✓	
GNUMERIC	319,137		✓	
NAUTILUS	129,439	✓	✓	✓
RHYTHMBOX	59,569	✓		✓
SPIM	20,300			

B. Liblit: Cooperative Bug Isolation, LNCS 4440, pp. 39–54, 2007.
© Springer-Verlag Berlin Heidelberg 2007

The design of a CBI system involves interesting challenges, both technical and social. In the next several sections, we focus on the solutions to technical problems most likely to be useful to the designers of similar systems and experiments: integration with existing native compilers (Sect. 3.1), management of static and dynamic linkage (Sect. 3.2), and correct execution in the presence of threads (Sect. 3.3).

Moving toward the social domain, Sect. 3.4 discusses the privacy and security facets of widespread monitoring of deployed software. Section 3.5 considers CBI from the user's perspective, and presents our approach to ensuring that users remain fully informed about and fully in control of their participation in the CBI system.

Lastly, Sect. 3.6 briefly reviews the current status of our public deployment, and offers general information about the state of this experiment under way.

3.1 Native Compiler Integration

The instrumentor as a whole looks and behaves like a C compiler with a few extra command line flags. It specifically emulates GCC, giving us easy access to a large corpus of open source applications. No manual annotation of source code is required, and all existing configuration scripts and makefiles work transparently. This design lets us instrument millions of lines of open source code and keep up with new releases with very short turnaround. Simply changing an environment variable ($CC) builds an application with our instrumenting compiler instead of the standard one.

The meat of instrumentation happens as a source to source transformation after the preprocessor and before the real C compiler. However, we actually need to affect all stages of compilation:

before preprocessing (cpp0): Pull in extra headers to declare or define various constructs used by instrumented code. For fixed content it is easier to use fixed headers rather than synthesizing the needed constructs programmatically within the instrumentor.

before compilation (cc1): Add sampled instrumentation as a source-to-source transformation. Emit additional static site information into temporary files for use in next step.

after assembly (asm): Fuse extra static site information from temporary files into the assembled object file.

before linking (ld): Pull in extra libraries containing common runtime support code and data used by instrumented programs.

We use GCC's -B <path> flag to specify an alternate directory in which to find the compiler stages. Custom scripts in that directory named cc1 and asm do the extra "before compilation" and "after assembly" work and invoke the corresponding native compiler stages as appropriate.

We also use GCC's -specs=<file> flag to augment (but not replace) the standard option specs file with one of our own. An *option specs file*, or simply "specfile," determines how GCC parses its command line arguments. We can add flags of our own, request temporary file names, and so on. A specfile is essentially a tiny domain-specific language for tweaking the command lines used for the various compiler stages. Using this facility we are able to take care of our "before preprocessing" and "before linking" needs by augmenting the cpp0 and ld command lines without actually replacing those stages with custom scripts of our own.

Starting in release 3.3, GCC has moved away from having a standalone cpp0 preprocessor stage. Instead the preprocessor is integrated into the main cc1 C compiler. On platforms without a cpp0, our replacement cc1 script invokes the real cc1 twice: once to preprocess the original source code and a second time to compile the transformed source after instrumentation has been added.

3.1.1 Static Site Information

While the main "before compilation" task is to inject instrumentation code, this phase also produces static reference information about each instrumentation site. This information includes each site's source file name, line number, host function, control flow graph node, and other properties specific to the instrumentation scheme being used. When decoding feedback reports, this information is used to tie predicate counts back to source level features understood by the programmer. Our experience is that maintaining this information external to the corresponding object file is brittle, as existing application build scripts often move or rename object files during the build process. Therefore, we fuse the static site information into the assembled object file by storing it in several custom ELF sections.

When the linker combines several object files, it pads each unknown section out to some fixed modulus and then concatenates all same-named sections in link order. We represent our static site information in a way that remains valid under null-byte injection and concatenation. Thus each instrumented executable, shared library, or plugin is self describing, with complete static information for all of its own instrumentation sites. Our extra sections are flagged as debug information, which means that they will be stripped out along with other debugging information during post-build packaging. We retain a copy locally to assist in report decoding, but end users do not need to download and store this extra information on their own machines.

3.2 Libraries and Plugins

Post-run reporting would be easy for an application that consisted of a single object file. We would simply write out the predicate counters in the order in which they appear in that file, and that list would constitute a complete report.

However, as seen in Table 3.1, many applications involve multiple object files in the form of shared libraries, plugins, or both. Note that this table counts only those shared libraries and plugins that are part of the source code of the application; additionally, there generally will be other shared libraries and plugins that are resident only on the end user's machine. Thus, the running environment is a mix of code that has been instrumented by CBI and code that we have never seen before. Shared libraries are also interesting because they may be used by other applications that we have not instrumented. Thus, not only must instrumented applications cope with uninstrumented code, but instrumented code must cope with finding itself in an uninstrumented application.

An orthogonal set of problems arises from static linking and dynamic loading. Our system does not have control over the linker and cannot assume that object files appear in any particular order. Plugins may be loaded late and unloaded at any time. If an instrumented plugin is about to be unloaded, we must capture its part of the feedback report immediately, because once it is unloaded its global predicate counters vanish from the address space and can no longer be accessed.

Our solution to all of these problems is to make each object file self-managing, with some initialization code that runs when it is loaded, and finalization code that runs when it is unloaded. For objects that are part of the main application binary, the initialization code runs early in program execution, before main. The finalization code runs after main returns or after exit is called. Shared libraries are similar. For plugins, the initialization code runs within dlopen after the plugin has been mapped into memory. Plugin finalization code runs within dlclose just before the plugin is removed from memory. Each object file also maintains its own instrumentation state; in particular, each object file maintains its own predicate counters.

All instrumented code shares a small amount of global state, such as the next-sample countdown and a random number generator. This state is initialized using the same early-execution facilities just before any instrumented object file is initialized. If the first piece of instrumented code is an external plugin, then the global shared state will be initialized when that plugin is first loaded. Thus, instrumented code still behaves as intended even when loaded up by an otherwise uninstrumented host application.

Self-management works well, but there is one situation in which we need global knowledge of the loaded object files. Finalization code does not run after a crash. Thus if the program receives a fatal signal, we must immediately gather the predicate counters from each loaded object file for the feedback report. We maintain a doubly-linked list of loaded object files, and the initialization/finalization code for each object file adds/removes that file from this list. Thus at any moment in time the application has a central registry of all instrumented, currently loaded object files.

We have also given some attention to the fact that this global registry could itself be corrupted by a buggy program. We maintain a global count of the expected size of the global registry. When walking the list in a signal handler, we use the counter to decide when to stop even if we have not reached the end of the list data structure. This extra check prevents an infinite loop if a memory error in the application introduces a cycle into the doubly-linked list. The global registry can be damaged in other ways by a misbehaving program, of course, but avoiding cycles is the most important case to handle.

The complications in checking for a corrupted global registry are just an example of the general problem that it is not possible to completely isolate program instrumentation from the program itself in unsafe languages such as C and C++. As a result it is necessary to sanity check feedback reports at the central server and discard any that are ill-formed. We do actually receive ill-formed reports, but the number is only a tiny fraction of all reports.

3.3 Threads

Nearly half of the applications listed in Table 3.1 are multi-threaded. Our CBI system maintains three kinds of global runtime data that need special attention in such software. In each case thread-safety can hurt performance, so we only take these extra measures if in fact the application is multi-threaded (e.g., if the compiler's command line contains the GCC -pthread flag).

3.3.1 Next-Sample Countdown

The most obvious piece of shared state is the next-sample countdown. In a multi-threaded system, the global variable holding this next-sample countdown would be a source of high contention among threads. Furthermore, our practice of caching the global countdown in local variables can easily lead to the same sort of coordination complications present in any multiprocessing system with per-processor caches.

A simple solution to this problem is to give each thread its own, independent countdown variable. This duplication is equivalent to giving each thread its own coin to toss. The behavior of the system with per-thread countdowns is indistinguishable from having a single global countdown, but avoids locking.

Enacting this plan requires compiler support. We use the __thread storage qualifier to declare thread-specific storage. This qualifier is a GCC extension and also requires support from the POSIX threading runtime, C library, and runtime loader. We also must alter thread creation so we can initialize the new thread's global state. We use the --wrap flag provided by the GNU linker to replace pthread_create with our augmented version.

3.3.2 Predicate Counters

The second class of data that requires special handling in multi-threaded applications is the predicate counters. Recall that the predicate counters keep track of how often a particular predicate at a particular line of code is observed to be true or false. For efficiency we use low sampling rates, such as once every hundred times (on average, randomized) that the line of code associated with the predicate is executed. Therefore predicates are tested rarely and any individual counter is accessed rarely even by a single thread. Consequently, we maintain only one copy of each predicate counter, shared by all threads. The critical operation on these counters, an increment by one, is so basic that every CPU architecture has some way of doing it atomically without resorting to heavyweight locking. For example, on the popular Intel IA-32 (a.k.a. x86) architecture, a LOCK-prefixed INC instruction gives exactly the desired behavior [35].

3.3.3 Compilation Unit Registry and Report File

The third class of data that must be protected from concurrent access includes the global registry of compilation units and the report file. These structures are only accessed when instrumented code is loaded or unloaded from the program's address space. Contention is expected to be low, and the performance impact of any reasonable solution small. We guarantee exclusive access by guarding each of these structures with its own conventional mutual exclusion lock.

3.3.4 Time Stamp Clock

The global clock used when time stamping samples (Sect. 2.2.3) is accessed every time a sample is taken, not every time a site is reached. Thus contention, while high, is lower than it would be for a shared global next-sample countdown. Our current implementation guards the clock with a conventional mutual exclusion lock. This design has the unfortunate effect of putting lock operations into the main sequence of program operations. The positive effect is that we retain a single, globally agreed upon clock for all samples in all threads. A possible alternative approach would be to use per-thread clocks akin to the per-thread next-sample countdowns discussed earlier. This design removes locks but sacrifices global ordering. Techniques for creating partially or totally ordered logical clocks in asynchronous distributed systems may also be applicable here.

3.3.5 Performance Evaluation

Table 2.1 and Fig. 2.2 used non-thread-safe instrumentation. Figure 3.1 shows how overheads grow or shrink when thread-safe instrumentation is used. (The underlying benchmarks used here are still single-threaded.) We note considerable increase in overhead at dense sampling rates and with the aggressive scalar-pairs instrumentation scheme. At sparser rates the effect is smaller but the trend remains. Thread-safe instrumentation does incur a performance cost. The fact that the cost is largest for the densest sampling rates suggests that the atomic increment instructions are a bottleneck. The problem may not be with the instructions themselves, but rather with the C compiler's ability to optimize code around them. We inject the increments using GCC extensions for inline assembly language. There are limits to how much information we can provide to the GCC optimizer about the behavior of these assembly fragments. To the extent that GCC treats the fragments as semantically opaque, GCC's optimizer must be more conservative than it would be if given pure C code. An instrumentor implementation based on binary rewriting would avoid this problem and therefore should be able to substantially reduce the cost of thread safety.

3.4 Privacy and Security

We have argued that the most important program behaviors are those exhibited by deployed software in the hands of users. However, any scheme for monitoring software post-deployment necessarily raises privacy and security concerns. The issues

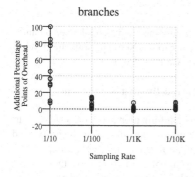

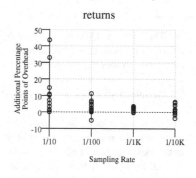

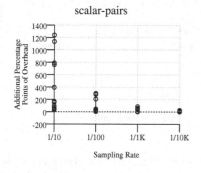

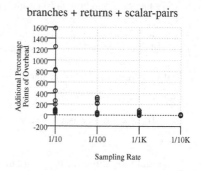

Fig. 3.1. Change in overhead with thread-safe instrumentation. Positive numbers indicate larger overhead relative to typical configuration.

are complex and as much social as technical. However, our approach can only succeed if users feel safe contributing to the shared data pool. Thus, addressing these concerns is both a moral and a practical imperative.

The experiences of Mozilla and Netscape with crash feedback systems may be illustrative. We have met with members of the Netscape Talkback Team, a group of quality assurance engineers who manage crash reports from the automated feedback system. Considerable effort has gone into designing the client side of this system so that users are fully informed. The system is strictly opt-in on a per-failure basis, or may be disabled entirely. The user may optionally examine the contents of the crash report, and no information is ever sent to Netscape without explicit authorization. Figure 3.2 shows the sort of information presented each time Netscape or Mozilla has crash data to submit.

Not all users will read or understand these assurances. Even so, there are some technical measures we can take to protect the privacy of even non-technically savvy users. The very nature of the sampling process itself affords a degree of anonymity. We collect a small bit of information from many, many users; any single run has little revelatory power.

> The Netscape Quality Feedback Agent is a feature that gathers predefined technical information about Communicator and sends it back to the Netscape software development team so they can improve future versions of Communicator.
>
> ...
>
> No information is sent until you can examine exactly what is being sent.
>
> ...
>
> Information gathered by this agent is limited to information about the state of Communicator when it has an error. Other sensitive information such as web sites visited, email messages, email addresses, passwords, and profiles will not be collected.
>
> All information Netscape collects via this agent will be used only for the purposes of fixing product defects and improving the quality of Netscape Communicator. This data is for internal diagnostic purposes only and will not be shared with third parties.
>
> For more information on Netscape's general privacy policy, go to: `<http://home.netscape.com/legal_notices/privacy.html>`
>
> Communicator activates the agent dialog box when a problem occurs, or when it has gathered information that Netscape needs to improve future versions of Communicator.
>
> ...
>
> If you prefer to disable the agent, you may do so here:

Fig. 3.2. Privacy assurances as used in Netscape Quality Feedback Agent

Some data, or some parts of execution, may be so sensitive that even this diffuse information leakage is unacceptable. Several type-based analyses under the broad heading of secure information flow [7, 60, 64] may be helpful here. Such systems statically identify parts of a program that manipulate sensitive data; we can avoid inserting instrumentation that reveals such values. Of course, this blacklisting will make it difficult to track bugs in security-sensitive parts of an application, but that trade-off is always present: one can only fix bugs about which the customer is willing to provide useful information.

A statistical approach designed to cope with noise offers some protection against malicious users who might try to poison the central database with bogus data, or overwhelm it with data representing the particular bugs they wish to see fixed. Recent work on protecting privacy and preventing abuse in collaborative filtering systems may also be applicable [10, 13].

3.5 User Interaction

When a user launches an instrumented application, he does not run the instrumented binary directly. Instead, we install a wrapper script in the expected location (e.g., /usr/bin) and put the instrumented binary elsewhere. The wrapper script has several responsibilities: it performs all user interaction that goes beyond what the underlying application would normally do, and it collects the raw feedback report from the instrumented application, packages it for transit, and sends it to the report collec-

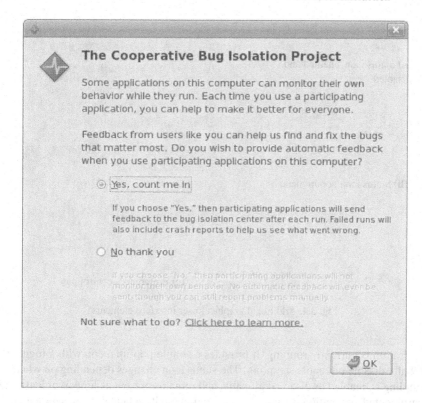

Fig. 3.3. First-time opt-in dialog box

tion server along with other information such as program outcome. In this way we avoid adding GUI infrastructure and encrypted networking support to the applications themselves. Also, the script can be in a different language, Python, which has excellent library support for both networking and desktop interaction.

When the wrapper script starts up, it checks whether the user has run an instrumented version of any application before. If not, it presents the first-time opt-in dialog box shown in Fig. 3.3. The dialog box briefly describes the goals of the project and the consequences of participating or not, and lets the user decide what to do. The logo icon and highlighting of the yes/no explanatory text change to reflect the user's current choice. A hyperlink button links to the project web site for more information [39]. This dialog box is initially presented in the background, and the real application launched without waiting for a reply. On this first run, the application reports no data. Once the user has selected yes or no, that preference is remembered and the first-time opt-in dialog box is not shown on subsequent runs, though it is possible to change the preference later using a distinct sampler control panel.

Also in the background, the wrapper posts a small status icon in the desktop status bar notification area. This icon provides a visual reminder that an instrumented

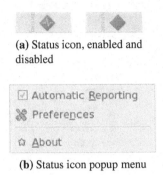

(a) Status icon, enabled and disabled

(b) Status icon popup menu

(c) Preferences control panel

Fig. 3.4. Additional graphical user interface elements

application is currently running. It provides a simple pop-up menu with a toggle to globally disable or enable sampling. The status icon changes depending on whether sampling is enabled or disabled globally, and remains present as long as at least one instrumented application is running. A second menu item launches the sampler control panel that allows for more detailed customization of data collection preferences. These additional graphical user interface elements are shown in Fig. 3.4.

The opt-in dialog box, status icon, and control panel work together to keep the user fully informed and fully in control. Additional configuration management hooks let system administrators change both defaults as well as mandatory, locked-down settings. These settings can include the sampling density, the address of the report collection server, and whether reporting is enabled for all or selected applications. Tracking of user behavior is a delicate matter, so users and their system administrators must be able to adapt the system to local needs and concerns.

Because the wrapper script launches the instrumented binary as a subprocess, it can also check that subprocess's exit status (either a result code or a fatal signal), which is included in the report uploaded to our feedback collection server. The wrapper script compresses the raw feedback report for transit using gzip-compatible compression. Compression is a huge benefit, as reports are mostly zeros and compress very well. The average compression of the reports we have received is 96%; Table 3.2 shows the range of report sizes we have received by application. The largest reports are less than forty kilobytes, which can be uploaded over even a slow modem connection in seconds.

Before submitting a report, the wrapper checks once more whether sampling is enabled both globally and for this application. If the user changed his or her mind

Table 3.2. Feedback report sizes

| Application | Size in Bytes | | |
	Min	Mean	Max
EVOLUTION	704	17,674	39,863
GAIM	1,786	12,072	27,809
THE GIMP	13,316	18,913	32,050
GNUMERIC	6,661	8,786	15,876
NAUTILUS	2,426	4,330	11,572
RHYTHMBOX	332	2,296	8,273
SPIM	198	833	2,184

after program launch, this second check gives the user a second chance to quash an unwanted feedback report before it reaches the collection server.

A report is submitted using an HTTP POST request across an encrypted SSL connection. Each HTTP request can also have a response from the server. Ordinarily the collection server does not give any response beyond a success code. However, if the server does give a response, the wrapper script receives it and presents it to the user as an HTML page. This feature might be used, for example, if a critical security issue were found requiring immediate upgrades.

The HTTP reply can also include a few special reply headers that update the local sampling configuration on the client. We have the ability to promote a different destination URL for future reports, which may be useful if we need to relocate the collection server. We can change the sampling density from its default of $1/100$, which may be useful if performance problems arise. We can also issue a "poison pill" that turns off sampling for future runs of the application. This facility is intended as a shutoff should the Cooperative Bug Isolation project be discontinued at some future date (a feature we learned would be useful from the prior experience of Elbaum and Hardojo [17]), and it might also be used to suppress future reports from individual misbehaving users. So far we have not needed any of these facilities.

3.6 Status of the Public Deployment

We conclude with some discussion of our experience thus far with our public deployment of the applications listed earlier.

3.6.1 Resource Requirements

One concern is that our approach adds a great deal of new code to an application; in fact, binaries will often be at least twice as large as the original, uninstrumented program. However, the growth in disk footprint is considerably smaller if one considers the entire package that comes with a typical large application, and in fact the

Table 3.3. Number of reports received to date

Application	Total	Good	Error	Crash
EVOLUTION	1,889	1,780	65	44 (2%)
GAIM	858	730	77	51 (6%)
THE GIMP	219	213	3	3 (1%)
GNUMERIC	294	275	2	17 (6%)
NAUTILUS	1,635	1,404	217	14 (1%)
RHYTHMBOX	1,520	1,326	69	125 (8%)
SPIM	1,066	393	670	3 (0%)

executable code is often a relatively small percentage of the total distribution. For the applications we have instrumented, downloaded packages are between 13% and 49% larger and the installed footprint on disk grows between 13% and 71%. The actual application binaries are between 74% and 304% larger than in the original distribution. Thus far we have received no complaints about package sizes, either downloaded or as expanded onto disk.

Another potential issue is application performance, but thus far we have received no complaints about the performance of any of our instrumented applications. We use 1/100 sampling, which apparently is sparse enough; we probably could have sampled even more densely for interactive applications that spend most of their time waiting for the user to do something. However, even these applications do have CPU-intensive phases, such as when RHYTHMBOX is loading up a library with thousands of music files or when GNUMERIC is recalculating a very large spreadsheet.

3.6.2 Reporting Trends

Table 3.3 summarizes the current state of the feedback data for each of our instrumented applications. The *total* number of valid feedback reports received so far is broken out into *good* runs, runs that exited with a non-zero *error* status, and runs that ended in a *crash* due to a fatal signal. Note the large variation in crash rates, from 0% (SPIM) to 8% (RHYTHMBOX). These overall failure rates may seem high, but they are well in line with rates observed in commercial software. A study of 1.3 million business computers found that 8% of Microsoft Windows sessions ended in failures requiring system reboots. Newer may not be better: the overall 8% rate breaks down as 3% for Windows NT, 4% for Windows 2000, and 12% for Windows XP [46].

There is both good news and bad news in the figures of Table 3.3. The bad news is that we have not yet received enough reports to carry out statistically significant analysis of the results, based on our previous experience with studies done "in the lab" running applications on synthetic data to simulate a large user community. Based on case studies in given in Chap. 4, we need tens of thousands of runs with our current methods to achieve accurate analysis of the results. This is at least

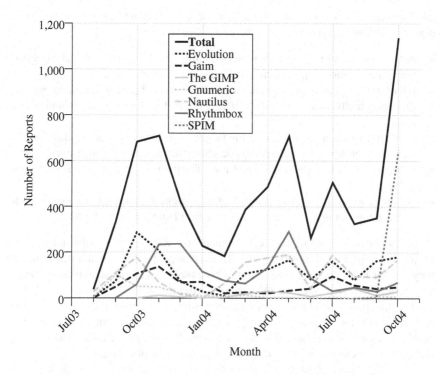

Fig. 3.5. Reports received per month and application

ten times the number of reports we have received to date for any of these applications. Our situation here reflects an inherent aspect of CBI and similar approaches, which is that these methods work well only beyond a certain minimum scale.

The good news is that these applications do crash, indicating to us that there is potential to improve the state of the software given enough users participating in CBI. In addition, we have enough data to demonstrate that the complete system works, from instrumenting code through gathering of reports, and we continue to receive new feedback reports daily. We are only at the beginning of this experiment and have not yet invested much effort in attracting users. The next step in our experiment will be to find ways to recruit enough users to test the advantages of CBI for large user communities of complex applications.

Popularity of Applications

Figure 3.5 shows how many reports have been received each month for each application since the public deployment began. The public deployment began with just four applications: EVOLUTION, GAIM, THE GIMP, and NAUTILUS. Other applications have been added over time. RHYTHMBOX was first made available in October of

2003 and quickly became one of our most heavily used (and most unstable) offerings. We attribute this popularity to several related factors:

- As is common in the open source community, the RHYTHMBOX developers do not make binaries available directly. They only provide source.
- RHYTHMBOX has many dependencies on external shared libraries. In practice, this complexity makes RHYTHMBOX difficult for novice users to build from source.
- RHYTHMBOX is a fairly high profile project. It is under very active development and fills a longstanding need for music library management on the Linux desktop.
- Until recently, the popular Red Hat Linux distributions did not include RHYTHMBOX binaries.
- At our request, the RHYTHMBOX web site suggests that users seeking binaries use those available from our Cooperative Bug Isolation project page.

These factors combine to create demand for RHYTHMBOX binaries that our project is uniquely well positioned to fill. Several people have mentioned to us that they use our RHYTHMBOX builds simply because that is the most convenient way to stay current with new releases. In short, we found a niche.

EVOLUTION and NAUTILUS are an interesting counterpoint. These applications are standard parts of nearly all modern Linux distributions. Our instrumented rebuilds provide no direct benefit to the user in the form of newer code or added functionality. Yet these are our two most heavily reported applications.

EVOLUTION and NAUTILUS are distinctive in being what we might call "session" applications: each typically starts when the user logs in and remains running until the user logs out. We only receive reports from session applications when users log out or when those applications crash. Therefore we had expected to see fewer EVOLUTION and NAUTILUS reports, and to see higher crash rates in the reports we did receive. In fact, the opposite is the case. What these two applications lack in start/stop cycles they make up for in ubiquity. A user might never run GNUMERIC during a given session, but if the user has logged in at all, then we *will* get one NAUTILUS report at the end of that session.

SPIM is the most recent addition to the application pool, first posted in September 2004. The sharp spike at the right edge of Fig. 3.5 shows that it has recently become extremely popular. This sudden popularity seems odd for such a specialized application. SPIM is a MIPS32 simulator: not the sort of thing most users need on a daily basis. By design we do not know who our users are; we do not even record the originating IP address of each report. However, the HTTPS server that receives reports keeps a rotating four-week access log. Inspection of this log, along with a few web searches, strongly suggests that our SPIM spike is associated with multiple students at the University of Innsbruck in Austria taking a class in computer architecture (*Rechnerarchitektur*). SPIM is used in this class, and the main SPIM web page directs Linux users to our project page for SPIM binary downloads. Thus we see again that referrals from developers' project pages are an important source of users for our public deployment.

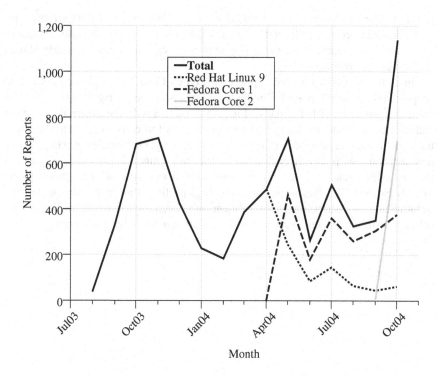

Fig. 3.6. Reports received per month and distribution

Popularity of Distributions

Unlike Windows or MacOS, Linux is packaged and released by multiple distributors. Figure 3.6 shows how many reports we have received each month for each supported distribution since the public deployment began.

The public deployment initially provided binaries only for Red Hat Linux 9. We selected this distribution because of its large user base and because of this author's familiarity with the technical particulars of that platform. In May 2004 we switched development to Fedora Core 1 and announced that Red Hat Linux 9 would no longer be updated.[1] We do still receive a significant number of Red Hat Linux 9 reports, presumably from users who decided to stop upgrading and stay with this well-regarded, fairly stable distribution.

While Fedora Core 1 saw rapid adoption in May and April of 2004, Red Hat Linux 9 reports dropped off at the same time. This shift suggests that most of the Fedora Core 1 users were existing Red Hat Linux 9 users who upgraded rather than new users joining our project for the first time. We observe as well that the sharp rise

---

[1] Names and numbers are deceiving: Fedora Core 1 is actually the direct successor to Red Hat Linux 9.

in Fedora Core 1 reports in July 2004 coincides with a drop-off of RHYTHMBOX reports. Fedora Core 1 includes RHYTHMBOX binaries. Although our builds are newer and more feature rich, easy availability of vendor-supplied binaries clearly shrank demand for our rebuilds.

In October 2004 we added support for Fedora Core 2, though we continue to support Fedora Core 1 as well. The Fedora Core 2 spike at the right edge of Fig. 3.6 coincides with the SPIM spike in Fig. 3.5, so apparently the Austrian computer architecture students are using Fedora Core 2. It is too early to tell whether other users are switching or whether new users are arriving. One challenge when adding new distributions is that it is difficult to stir up as much interest as we got with the first public releases. Our August 2003 launch saw articles in Slashdot, Linux Weekly News, CNET News.com, and other high profile online technology news fora. Subsequent new distribution announcements have been limited to mailing lists for the relevant distributions and applications, which are much smaller audiences.

4

Techniques for Statistical Debugging

> *What is luck? Luck is probability taken personally. It is the*
> *excitement of bad math.*
>
> *–Penn Jillette*

Thus far we have focused on techniques for collecting sparsely sampled data from large numbers of users. However, this data is only as good as the sense we can make of it. This chapter presents several techniques for using sparsely sampled data to isolate the causes of bugs.

Sampled data is terribly incomplete. With $1/100$ sampling, 99% of everything that happens is not even seen. Thus, we do not give strict causes and effects as one might look for using a symbolic debugger. Instead we use statistical models to identify those behaviors that tend to be strongly predictive of failure over many runs. We refer to this body of techniques as *statistical debugging*. Statistical debugging reaps the benefits of the Bernoulli sampling transformation developed in Sect. 2.1.1. While the data is incomplete, it is incomplete in a fair, statistically unbiased way. Thus the observed data is a noisy but representative sample of the complete behavior, and failure trends identified in the former are equally applicable to the later.

Section 4.1 defines some basic notation and terminology that we will use throughout the remainder of this chapter. In Sect. 4.2 we describe an algorithm for isolating single, deterministic bugs using a process of elimination. Section 4.3 extends our scope to non-deterministic bugs using a general-purpose statistical regression model. This approach has certain limitations, which we discuss in greater depth in Sect. 4.3.4 and Sect. 4.4. Better understanding of these limitations leads us to develop an improved algorithm in Sect. 4.5 that combines statistical ranking techniques with an iterative bug elimination process to manage multiple unknown deterministic and non-deterministic bugs. The ranking and iterative elimination is our best known algorithm to date. Section 4.6 offers several case studies demonstrating how the algorithm has been used to successfully isolate both known and previously unknown bugs in real applications.

4.1 Notation and Terminology

Let $\mathcal{P}$ represent the set of all fundamental and inferred predicates for a given program. A feedback report R consists of one bit indicating whether a run of the program

B. Liblit: Cooperative Bug Isolation, LNCS 4440, pp. 55–88, 2007.
© Springer-Verlag Berlin Heidelberg 2007

succeeded or failed, as well as a vector with one counter for each predicate $P \in \mathcal{P}$. Let $R(P)$ represent the counter value for P in R. If P is observed to be true during at least once run R, then $R(P) > 0$; if P is never observed to be true during run R, then $R(P) = 0$.

Predicates arise from instrumentation sites. Let S be an instrumentation site. As a notational shorthand, define the count of a site $R(S)$ to be the sum of the counts of its constituent fundamental predicates. Note that for all of the instrumentation schemes described in Sect. 2.2, the set of fundamental predicates arising from a site form a partition of the set of all possible program states at that site. Thus, one observation at a site S entails one true observation of exactly one fundamental predicate $P \in S$. Conversely, if $R(S) = 0$, then site S must never have been observed.

Let B denote a bug (i.e., something that causes incorrect behavior in a program). We use $\mathcal{B}$ to denote a *bug profile*, i.e., a set of failing runs (feedback reports) that share a cause of failure. The meaning becomes clear in context. The union of all bug profiles is exactly the set of failing runs, but note that $\mathcal{B}_i \cap \mathcal{B}_j \neq \emptyset$ in general; more than one bug can occur in some runs.

A predicate P is a *bug predictor* (or simply a *predictor*) of bug B if whenever $R(P) > 0$ then it is statistically likely that $R \in \mathcal{B}$ (see Sect. 4.5.1). The goal of statistical debugging is to select a small subset $\mathcal{A} \subseteq \mathcal{P}$ such that $\mathcal{A}$ has predictors of all bugs. Ideally we would also like to rank the predictors in $\mathcal{A}$ from the most to least important according to some reasonable definition of "importance." The set $\mathcal{A}$ and associated metrics are then available to engineers to help speed the process of finding and fixing the most serious bugs.

It is occasionally useful to distinguish deterministic from non-deterministic bugs. A bug is *deterministic* with respect to a predicate P if whenever P is true, the program is guaranteed to crash at some future point. A bug is *non-deterministic* with respect to a set of program predicates if it is not deterministic for any predicate in the set (i.e., none of the considered predicates perfectly predicts program crashes).

4.2 Predicate Elimination

We begin with automatic isolation of deterministic bugs with the additional simplifying assumption that each program under analysis has only one bug. Deterministic bugs are quite common, though they are generally easier to find and fix using any method than non-deterministic bugs (see Sect. 4.3).

4.2.1 Instrumentation Strategy

As a case study in finding deterministic bugs we take release 1.2 of the CCRYPT encryption tool. This version is known to contain a bug that involves overwriting existing files. If the user responds to a confirmation prompt with EOF rather than yes or no, CCRYPT crashes.

The EOF sensitivity suggests that the problem has something to do with CCRYPT's interactions with standard file operations. In C, these functions commonly return values to indicate success or failure. We therefore choose to instrument CCRYPT using the returns instrumentation scheme discussed in Sect. 2.2.2. Thus, when an instrumented run terminates, we can examine any function call of interest and ask how often that call was observed to return a negative, zero, or positive value.

For CCRYPT, there are 570 call sites of interest, for $570 \times 3 = 1,710$ counters. Each counter corresponds to a single predicate that is hypothesized to behave differently in successful versus crashed runs. Specifically, we pose the problem as follows:

> Assume that predicates capture incorrect behavior. That is, assume that each predicate P should always be false during correct execution. When P is true, the program either fails (a deterministic bug) or is at increased risk of failing (a non-deterministic bug).

If we eliminate all predicates for which this hypothesis is disproved by observed runtime behavior, then the predicates that remain describe the conditions under which the program fails.

4.2.2 Elimination Strategies

We make no effort to restrict instrumentation to known system or library calls, nor do we distinguish functions that return status codes from those that do not. Most of those 1,710 predicates, then, have no bearing on program success or failure. Given a set of runs, we can discard irrelevant predicates using a set of *elimination strategies*:

⟨**Elimination by universal falsehood**⟩: Disregard any predicate P such that $R(P) = 0$ on all runs R. P likely represents a predicate that can never be true.

⟨**Elimination by lack of failing coverage**⟩: Disregard all predicates for a site S if $R(S) = 0$ on all failed runs R. Because one counter in each triple must always be true for any sample, these predicates likely arise from an instrumentation site that is not even reached in failing executions.

⟨**Elimination by lack of failing example**⟩: Disregard any predicate P such that $R(P) = 0$ on all failed runs R. P likely represents a predicate that need not be true for a failure to occur.

⟨**Elimination by successful counterexample**⟩: Disregard any predicate P such that $R(P) > 0$ on at least one successful run R. P must represent a predicate that can be true without causing a subsequent program failure.

We characterize these as strategies because they are subject to noise from random sampling, and also because not all are equally applicable to all bugs. For example, elimination by ⟨successful counterexample⟩ assumes that the bug is deterministic. The other three strategies do not make this assumption, but do require enough runs so that any predicate that is ever true is likely to have been observed true at least once. Note that these strategies are also not independent: ⟨universal falsehood⟩ and ⟨lack of failing coverage⟩ each eliminate a subset of the counters identified by ⟨lack of failing example⟩. Elimination strategies also vary in which kinds of runs they exploit: ⟨successful counterexample⟩ considers only successful runs; ⟨lack of failing example⟩ and ⟨lack of failing coverage⟩ consider only failures; ⟨universal falsehood⟩ uses both.

4.2.3 Data Collection and Analysis

In lieu of a large user community, we generate many runs artificially in the spirit of the Fuzz project [43]. Each run uses a randomly selected set of present or absent files, randomized command line flags, and randomized responses to CCRYPT prompts including the occasional EOF.

We have collected 2,990 trial runs at a sampling rate of $1/1,000$; 88 of these end in a crash. Applying each elimination strategy independently to the counter traces:

⟨**Universal falsehood**⟩ discards 1,569 counters that are zero on all runs, leaving 141 candidate predicates.

⟨**Lack of failing coverage**⟩ discards 526 counter triples that are all zero on all crashes, leaving 132 candidate predicates.

⟨**Lack of failing example**⟩ discards 1,665 counters that are zero on all crashes, leaving 45 candidate predicates.

⟨**Successful counterexample**⟩ discards 139 counters that are non-zero on any successful run, leaving 1,571 candidate predicates.

Several factors conspire to drive most counters to zero: the naïve nature of our guesses, the limited coverage of our automated test suite, and the filtering effect of sparse sampling. Thus, elimination by ⟨universal falsehood⟩ looks quite effective at first glance, while elimination by ⟨successful counterexample⟩ seems rather poor. However, these two strategies test disjoint properties and can be combined to good effect. The combination leaves only those predicates that are sometimes observed to be true in failed runs but never observed to be true in successful runs. For our CCRYPT trials, only two predicates meet these criteria:

```
1. traverse.c:320: file_exists return value > 0
2. traverse.c:122: xreadline return value == 0
```

Examining the corresponding code shows that these predicates are consistent with the circumstances under which the bug is reported to occur. This call to file_exists returns "1" when an output file already exists. A confirmation prompt is presented, and this call to xreadline returns the user's reply, or null if the input terminal is at EOF. Inspection of the code immediately following the xreadline call shows that the programmer forgot to check for the EOF case: he assumes that xreadline returns a non-null string, and immediately inspects its contents. We have successfully isolated this (known) bug in CCRYPT, and the fix is clear.

While the file_exists predicate is not itself the cause of the bug, the fact that it appears on our list is useful information. It represents a necessary condition under which crashes occur. That may be helpful, for example, if the engineer wishes to reproduce the bug in-house for further study. Of course, there should be some runs where file_exists reports that the file exists but xreadline returns a valid response from the user and therefore the program does not crash. If the file_exists call is sampled on any such run, elimination by ⟨successful counterexample⟩ correctly determines that this predicate does not imply failure. It will be eliminated from further consideration, and only the true "smoking gun," the call to xreadline, will remain. Thus we have the ability to identify not only the direct cause of a bug but also related behaviors that are strongly but imperfectly correlated with failure. We further explore this idea of broad correlation in Sect. 4.3, where even the buggy line of code itself does not always cause a crash.

As previously noted, the first three elimination strategies partially overlap, while the last, ⟨successful counterexample⟩, is distinct. ⟨Universal falsehood⟩ and ⟨successful counterexample⟩ only look at successful runs, hence are easily analyzed together. ⟨Lack of failing example⟩ in general eliminates the most features, and therefore is also a good candidate to combine with ⟨successful counterexample⟩. Doing so in the case of CCRYPT leaves us with exactly the same two features, though in general one might find different results. Elimination by ⟨lack of failing coverage⟩, on the other hand, is an inherently weaker strategy: when combined with ⟨successful counterexample⟩, we are still left with 86 features.

4.2.4 Refinement over time

In order to gain a better understanding of how the elimination strategies benefit from increasing the number of runs, we have experimented with randomized subsets of our complete run suite. We have seen that elimination by ⟨successful counterexample⟩ is quite effective when given a few thousand successful runs; how well does it perform with a smaller suite? We start with the 141 candidate predicates that are ever nonzero on any run. We assemble a random subset of fifty successful runs and filter the predicate set using elimination by ⟨successful counterexample⟩. We then add another fifty runs, and another fifty, and so on in steps up to the full set of 2,902 successful runs. We repeat this entire process one hundred times to gauge how rapidly one can expect the predicate set to shrink as more runs arrive over time.

Figure 4.1 shows the results. The crosses mark the mean number of predicates remaining, while the vertical bars extend one standard deviation above and below the mean. The short vertical bars in this case tells us that there is relatively little diversity in each of the hundred random subsets at any given size. The results show that, on average, 1,750 runs are enough to isolate twenty candidate features, another 500 runs reduces that count by half, and a total of 2,600 runs is enough to narrow the set of good features down to just five. One would expect more variety in runs collected from real users rather than an automated script. Greater diversity can only benefit the analysis, as it would provide more novel counterexamples and therefore may eliminate more uninteresting predicates more rapidly.

4.2.5 Performance Impact

Instrumenting function return values confounds several of the optimizations proposed in Sect. 2.3. If most function calls are instrumentation sites, and if most function calls terminate acyclic regions, then most acyclic regions contain only a single site and we have poor amortization of sampling overhead. Furthermore, CCRYPT is built one object file at a time, and we must conservatively assume that any cross-object function call is not weightless. Thus, for much of CCRYPT, our sampling

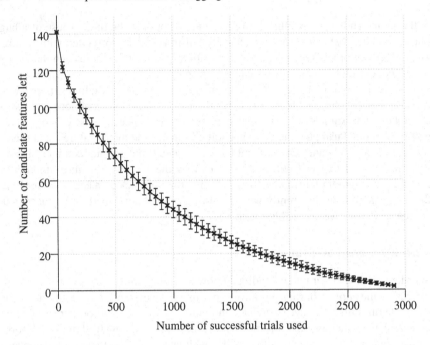

Fig. 4.1. Progressive elimination by ⟨successful counterexample⟩ as successful runs accumulate. Crosses mark means; error bars mark one standard deviation.

transformation devolves to a simpler but slower pattern of checking the next-sample countdown at each and every site.

In spite of this extra work, the performance impact of sampled instrumentation is minimal. We find that the overhead for $1/_{1,000}$ sampling in CCRYPT is less than 4%, and progressively sparser sampling rates shrink the overhead still further. Unconditional instrumentation also performs well here, making either reasonable for this particular application. In the next section, though, we consider a more invasive instrumentation strategy that requires sampling to keep overhead under control.

4.2.6 Limitations and Insights

Predictor selection using predicate elimination strategies is fundamentally dependent upon two assumptions: (1) that there is exactly one bug, and (2) that there is at least one completely deterministic predictor for this bug. If assumption (1) is untrue, then presumably even a perfect predictor for one bug will fail to consistently predict other bugs, effectively violating assumption (2). If assumption (2) is untrue, then even a single run in which the predictor was observed true but the program succeeded anyway will suffice to eliminate the predictor by ⟨successful counterexample⟩. Thus if there is no 100% deterministic predictor eventually all predicates will be eliminated.

Relaxing these requirements requires substantially different approaches, and we explore other options in the sections that follow. However this algorithm is a useful starting point because it serves to illustrate several key concepts common to all statistical debugging approaches. Chief among these is the idea of rapidly paring down a large set of mostly uninteresting predicates to find a much smaller set of true bug predictors. Also, it is useful for bug isolation algorithms to be progressive, yielding rough answers for few runs and successively more precise or more confident information as runs accumulate. Lastly, if we allow for less strict interpretations, the elimination strategies of Sect. 4.2.2 do describe generally desirable properties of bug predictors. Predicates that differ between successful and failing runs are interesting; those that do not differ are uninteresting. Good predictors should be true (or should tend to be true) in failing runs and should be false (or should tend to be false) in successful runs. Any approach to statistical debugging ultimately depends upon identifying differences in the behaviors of successful and failed runs.

4.3 Regularized Logistic Regression

In this section we consider the automatic isolation of non-deterministic bugs. Recall from Sect. 4.1 that a bug is non-deterministic with respect to a set of program predicates if no predicate in the set is perfectly correlated with program crashes. Thus non-determinacy is in part a function of what we choose to observe. If we treat the implementation of malloc et al. as opaque, then many C heap corruption bugs become non-deterministic with respect to all observed predicates.

For this case study we use version 1.06 of the GNU implementation of BC, a basic command-line calculator tool. We find that feeding BC nine megabytes of random input causes it to crash roughly one time in four from, as it turns out, a previously unknown buffer overrun error. Since BC sometimes terminates successfully even when it overruns the buffer, this bug is non-deterministic.

The scalar-pairs instrumentation scheme described in Sect. 2.2.2 can be useful for detecting boundary condition violations associated with buffer overruns. We instrument BC using the scalar-pairs scheme with variable-to-variable and variable-to-zero comparisons only. For BC this scheme induces 10,050 sites, or 30,150 predicate counters in all. The vast majority of these are of no interest: either they compare completely unrelated variables, or they express relationships that behave identically in both successful and failed runs. The challenge is to find the few predicates that matter. Because the bug is non-deterministic, if we have enough runs no predicates will satisfy elimination by ⟨successful counterexample⟩. Therefore we set aside this elimination strategy in favor of statistical modeling to identify behavior that is broadly correlated with failure.

4.3.1 Crash Prediction Using Logistic Regression

To find important but possibly non-deterministic predictors, we recast bug isolation as a statistical analysis problem. Each run of BC constitutes one sample point consisting of 30,150 observed *features* (counters) and one binary *outcome* (0 = succeeded, 1 = crashed). Given numerous data points (sampled runs), we want to identify a subset of our 30,150 features that predict the outcome. This problem is equivalent to the machine learning problem of learning a binary classifier with feature selection, i.e., using as few input features as possible.

In the classification setting, we take a set of data with known binary output (a training set), and attempt to learn a binary classifier that gives good predictions on a test set. The learning process usually involves additional parameters whose values can be determined using a cross-validation set. In our case, the end goal is to narrow down the set of features. Hence our method must balance good classification performance with aggressive feature selection.

A binary classifier takes feature values as inputs, and outputs a prediction of either 0 or 1. *Logistic regression* [28] is a method of learning a binary classifier where the output function is assumed to be logistic. The logistic function is a continuous "S"-shaped curve approaching 0 on one end, and 1 on the other. The output can be interpreted as a probability measure of how likely it is that the data point falls within class 0 or 1. Quantizing the logistic function output then gives us a binary classifier: if the output is greater than $1/2$, then the data point is classified as class 1 (a crash), otherwise it falls under class 0 (a successful run). Feature selection can be achieved by *regularizing* the function parameters to ignore most input features, forcing it to form a model that predicts success or failure using just a small selection of sampled features. Regularization is important for our purposes because we expect that most of our features are wild guesses, but that there may be just a few that correctly characterize the bug.

While other techniques for combined classification and feature selection exist, few of them are particularly well-suited for this problem. Some methods [24, 58] calculate a univariate correlation coefficient independently for each feature; other methods, such as decision trees [6], are more computationally intensive. In our dataset, the features are clearly not independent of each other, and the size of the problem can potentially be too large for more computationally intensive methods. Furthermore, logistic regression is a discriminative classification method, and thus does not make any assumptions about the underlying distribution of the input. This property is crucial since our features arise from a decidedly artificial process and would be difficult to characterize using simple distributions.

Suppose our training set $\mathcal{D}$ consists of M data points $(x_1, y_1), \ldots, (x_M, y_M)$, where each $x_i \in \mathcal{R}^N$ denotes a vector of input predicate counters, and each $y_i = \{0, 1\}$ denotes the corresponding output label. To learn a good classifier, we can maximize the *log likelihood* of the training set, defined as follows:

$$LL(\mathcal{D}) = \sum_{i=1}^{M} [y_i \log Pr(Y = 1|x)$$
$$+ (1 - y_i) \log(1 - Pr(Y = 1|x))].$$

Here the output labels y_i are used as indicator functions to zero out exactly one of the two terms in each summand. In logistic regression, the distribution $Pr(Y = 1|x)$ is modeled as the logistic function $\mu_{\tilde{\beta}}(x)$ with parameters $\tilde{\beta} = \langle \beta_0 \in \mathcal{R}, \beta \in \mathcal{R}^N \rangle$.

$$Pr(Y = 1|x) = \mu_{\tilde{\beta}}(x) = \frac{1}{1 + \exp(-\beta_0 - \beta^T x)}.$$

The logistic parameters β_0 and β take on the respective roles as the intercept and slope of the classifier, and essentially weigh the relative importance of each feature in the final outcome. We expect most of the input features to have no influence over the success or failure of the program, so we place an additional constraint that forces most of the β's toward zero. This constraint is implemented by subtracting a penalty term based on the ℓ_1 norm $\|\tilde{\beta}\|_1 = \sum_{j=0}^{M} |\beta_j|$. We can tune the importance of this *regularization term* through a *regularization parameter* λ. The penalized log likelihood function is:

$$LL(\tilde{\beta}|\mathcal{D}, \lambda) = \sum_{i=1}^{M} [y_i \log \mu_{\tilde{\beta}}(x_i) + (1 - y_i) \log(1 - \mu_{\tilde{\beta}}(x_i))]$$
$$- \lambda \|\tilde{\beta}\|_1.$$

An assignment of β coefficients that maximizes this function represents a model that maximizes the fidelity of its predictions while still limiting itself to form those predictions on the basis of only a small number of features from the complete feature set.

4.3.2 Data Collection and Analysis

Our BC data set consists of 4,390 runs with distinct random inputs and distinct randomized $1/1,000$ sampling. We randomly chose 2,729 runs for training, 322 runs for cross-validation, and 1,339 runs for testing. Although there are 30,150 raw features, many can be discarded immediately using elimination by ⟨universal falsehood⟩: in the training set 27,242 features are always zero. Hence the effective number of features used in training is 2908. (Elimination by ⟨lack of failing example⟩ can eliminate another 647 features that are zero for all failed runs. However we find that the presence or absence of these 647 features does not significantly affect the quality of the regularized logistic regression results.)

To make the magnitude of the β parameters comparable, the feature values must be on the same scale. Hence all the input features are shifted and scaled to lie on the interval $[0, 1]$, then normalized to have unit sample variance. A suitable value for the regularization parameter λ is determined through cross-validation to be 0.3. The model is then trained using stochastic gradient ascent to reach a local maximum of the penalized log likelihood. Using a step size of 10^{-5}, the model usually converges within sixty iterations through the training set. This process takes roughly thirty minutes in MATLAB on a 1.8 GHz Pentium 4 CPU with 1 GB of RAM.

Once the model has been trained, predicates with the largest β coefficients suggest where to begin looking for the bug. In our case, the top five ranked coefficients are well-separated in magnitude from the rest, and show an unmistakable trend:

```
152  void
153  more_arrays ()
154  {
155    int indx;
156    int old_count;
157    bc_var_array **old_ary;
158    char **old_names;
159
160    /* Save the old values. */
161    old_count = a_count;
162    old_ary = arrays;
163    old_names = a_names;
164
165    /* Increment by a fixed amount and allocate. */
166    a_count += STORE_INCR;
167    arrays = (bc_var_array **) bc_malloc (a_count*sizeof(bc_var_arra...
168    a_names = (char **) bc_malloc (a_count*sizeof(char *));
169
170    /* Copy the old arrays. */
171    for (indx = 1; indx < old_count; indx++)
172      arrays[indx] = old_ary[indx];
173
174
175    /* Initialize the new elements. */
176    for (; indx < v_count; indx++)
177      arrays[indx] = NULL;
178
179    /* Free the old elements. */
180    if (old_count != 0)
181      {
182        free (old_ary);
183        free (old_names);
184      }
185  }
```

Fig. 4.2. Suspect BC function more_arrays. All top-ranked crash-predicting features point to large values of indx on line 176.

1. storage.c:176: in function more_arrays: indx > scale
2. storage.c:176: in function more_arrays: indx > use_math
3. storage.c:176: in function more_arrays: indx > opterr
4. storage.c:176: in function more_arrays: indx > next_func
5. storage.c:176: in function more_arrays: indx > i_base

The source code for more_arrays appears in Fig. 4.2. A comment earlier in the same file suggests that this function is one of a suite of "three functions for increasing the number of functions, variables, or arrays that are needed." The logic is a fairly clear instance of the buffer reallocation idiom, even to one unfamiliar with the code: line 167 allocates a larger chunk of memory; line 171 is the top of a loop that copies values over from the old, smaller array; line 176 completes the resize by zeroing out the new extra space. As the comment suggests, there are two similar functions (more_functions and more_variables) nearby that do largely the same thing with different storage pools. The text of these three functions is nearly identical, but each uses different global variables (such as a_count versus f_count versus v_count).

The top ranked predicates seem bizarre on first examination, because the variables they relate do not appear to have any real connection to each other or to more_arrays. For example, scale tracks significant digits for floating point calculations, while use_math records whether an initial math library is to be loaded. Why would crashes tend to happen when local variable indx exceeds these seemingly unrelated globals on this particular line? An obvious hypothesis is that indx is simply unusually large in such cases. If indx is large, then it will tend to be larger than any number of otherwise unrelated variables. Perhaps crashes occur when the input to BC defines unusually large numbers of arrays.

Closer scrutiny of more_arrays quickly reveals this hypothesis to be true. The allocation on line 167 requests space for a_count items. The copying loop on line 171 ranges from 1 through old_count − 1. The zeroing loop on line 176 continues on from old_count through v_count − 1. And here we find the bug: the new storage buffer has room for a_count elements, but the second loop is incorrectly bound by v_count instead. After a glimpse at the neighboring more_variables function, it is clear that more_arrays was created by copying and pasting more_variables and then changing names like v_count and v_names to a_count and a_names. The loop bound on line 176 was overlooked in the renaming.

The logistic regression model points us at the buggy line, the buggy variable, and even reveals something of the conditions under which the bug appears. Having found the bug, it is reasonable to ask whether the statistical analysis could have pointed at it even more directly. The mistaken use of v_count instead of a_count on line 176 means that a buffer overrun occurs when indx > a_count on line 176. This condition does correspond to a predicate sampled by our system, but the predicate is ranked 240th in the trained model. Why was this smoking gun not ranked first?

There are several reasons to consider. Samples are taken randomly, while the model itself is trained using stochastic gradient ascent. Thus, a degree of noise is fundamental to the process. Even crashing is not guaranteed: out of 320 runs in which sampling spotted indx > a_count at least once, 66 did not crash. Thus, C programs can "get lucky", meaning that we do not have a strict overrun $\implies$ crash implication. Manual inspection of the data reveals a high degree of redundancy among many instrumentation sites within more_arrays, meaning that the model has several features to choose from that have equivalent predictive power. Our counters may be too fine-grained here: we are distinguishing many behaviors that are in fact so tightly interrelated as to be equivalent.

This bug seems clear enough once found. However it has been present and undiscovered at least since 1992 (the time stamp on this file in the oldest version of GNU

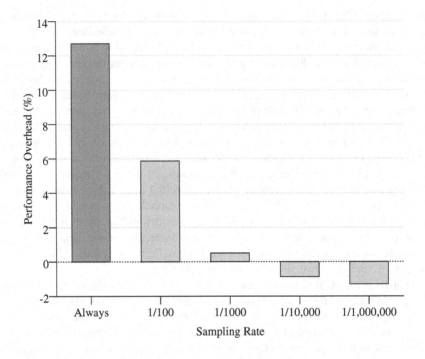

Fig. 4.3. Overhead of BC with unconditional or sampled instrumentation

BC that we can find). Many bugs are obvious only once one knows where to look. The logistic regression results directed us to one misbehaving variable on one line of code, out of 8910 lines in BC as a whole. Our approach does not automatically find and fix bugs. But it does suggest where to start looking, and what sort of scenarios (e.g., unusually large indx) to consider. Although we are still learning about the capabilities of this system and how to interpret its results, we believe that statistically guided debugging has the potential to make the process of finding and fixing bugs more efficient and more responsive to the needs of end users.

4.3.3 Performance Impact

Our BC instrumentation is fairly dense. The leftmost bar in Fig. 4.3 shows that if this instrumentation is added without sampling, the performance penalty is 13%. A sampling density of 1/100 cuts the penalty in half (6%). At the 1/1,000 density used in our statistical debugging experiment, the penalty is barely measurable (0.5%). Still lower densities show small speedups relative to uninstrumented code. This behavior is apparently due to effects such as changes in relative code alignment, cache behavior, measurement noise, and other unpredictable factors. Thus, we achieved an important goal: at least for this application, we can sample program behavior at densities that allow us to isolate real bugs while imposing an overhead on clients that is so small as to be unmeasurable in practice.

4.3.4 Limitations and Insights

Regularized logistic regression gives encouraging results for BC, a small program exhibiting a single bug. However, as we worked to apply these methods to much larger programs under realistic conditions we discovered a number of serious scalability problems:

- For large applications the set of candidate predicates numbers in the hundreds of thousands of predicates, many of which are, or are very nearly, logically redundant. In our experience, this redundancy causes regularized logistic regression to choose highly redundant lists of failure predictors. Redundancy is already evident in the list of BC failure predictors from Sect. 4.3.2. This problem becomes much worse for larger programs.
- A separate difficulty is the prevalence of predicates predicting multiple bugs. For example, for many Unix programs a bug is more likely to be encountered when many command line flags are given, because the more options that are given non-default settings the more likely unusual code paths are to be exercised. Thus, predicates implying a long command line may rank near the top, even though such predicates are useless for isolating the cause of individual bugs.
- Finally, different bugs occur at rates that differ by orders of magnitude. In reality, we do not know which failure is caused by which bug, so we are forced to lump all the bugs together and try to learn a binary classifier. Thus, predictors for all but the most common bugs have relatively little influence over the global optimum and tend to be ranked low or not included in the selected predictor list at all.

These problems with regularized logistic regression persist in many variations we have investigated, including approaches that use nonstandard utility functions to model the behavior of nondeterministic failures [65]. Analysis of this body of experimental work yielded some key technical insights. In addition to the bug predictors we wish to find among the instrumented predicates, there are several other kinds of predicates. First, nearly all predicates (often 98% or 99%) are not predictive of anything. These *non-predictors* are best identified and discarded as quickly as possible. Among the remaining predicates that can predict failure in some way, there are some bug predictors. There are also *super-bug predictors*: predicates that, as described above, predict failures due to a variety of bugs. And there are *sub-bug predictors*: predicates that characterize a subset of the instances of a specific bug; these are often special cases of more general problems.

4.4 MOSS: A Multiple-Bug Challenge

When a program contains multiple bugs, the difficulties created by super- and sub-bug predictors become pronounced. To assess the viability of regularized logistic regression in this context we performed an experiment in which we knew the set of bugs in advance. We chose MOSS [56] as our benchmark program. MOSS is a software plagiarism detection service[1]. It has been available since the late 1990's and has several thousand users worldwide. As such, MOSS has many of the characteristics of real software: it has users who depend on it, it is constantly undergoing revision as its purpose and the environment in which it runs evolves, and it is complex enough to be composed of several interacting subsystems.

The choice of how to inject bugs into software can be problematic, as the choice of bugs to include or exclude can dramatically affect the results. Nearly all of the bugs were taken directly from the bug logs for MOSS. In some cases the code had evolved since the original bug was fixed, in which case we had to judge how to modify the bug to inject it into the code. We also included three bugs that were not MOSS bugs. One of these is a known bug from another system where there is an obviously analogous place to add that bug to MOSS (see below). The other two are duplicates of two different buffer overrun bugs in MOSS. In each case, we restored the original bug, and then added a second, very similar buffer overrun in a different place, the purpose being to see if our algorithm could not only detect the overruns, but also distinguish between them.

We briefly describe the nine bugs we added to MOSS:

1. To correctly report the location of duplicate code MOSS must track line numbers. We introduced a bug that causes the number of lines in C-style multi-line comments to be counted incorrectly. The bug only occurs under a special set of circumstances: the option to match comments must be on (normally MOSS ignores comments completely, and that is a separate code path with no bug), the programs involved must have C multi-line comments, and in addition the position of these comments must ultimately affect the output. Note that this bug is not only non-deterministic in the sense defined in Sect. 4.1, it also does not cause the program to crash; the program simply generates incorrect output.

2. MOSS has the option to dump its internal data structures in a binary file format called a *database*. We removed the check for a null FILE pointer in the case that the database cannot be opened for writing. This bug is analogous to one reported in CCRYPT. It is a deterministic bug, and in fact the program crashes almost immediately after failing to open the file.

3. Loading a MOSS database is complex, as a number of data structures must be kept in sync. We removed an array bounds update in the database loading routine, so that even though a database was loaded, the pointer to the end of one array A was not moved to reflect that new data had been added to the end of A. The program behaves normally unless a second database is loaded, at which point the second database at least partially overwrites that portion of the first database stored in A. This bug has unpredictable effects. Depending on what files are compared and the contents of the databases loaded, the result might be that the

---

[1] That is, MOSS detects copying in large sets of programs. The typical MOSS user is a professor or teaching assistant in a programming course.

program terminates with correct output, that it terminates with incorrect output, or that it crashes. This bug was particularly difficult to find originally.

4. We removed a size check that prevented users from supplying command-line arguments that could cause the program to overrun the bounds of an array. When this bug is triggered the program may terminate with correct output, terminate with incorrect output, or crash.

5. For historical reasons, Moss handles Lisp programs differently from all other languages. The Lisp processing involves a standard hash table. We removed one of the end-of-bucket checks, which causes a crash when the program scans to the end of a hash bucket and tries to dereference a NULL pointer.

6. For efficiency Moss preallocates a large area of memory for its primary data structure. When this area of memory is filled, the program should fail gracefully. We removed the out-of-memory check. The original bug was more complex, but cannot be reproduced exactly because this portion of the code has been revised.

7. Moss has a routine that scans an array for multiple copies of a data value. We removed the limit check that prevents the code from searching past the end of the array. This bug is another buffer overrun, but of a different kind. First, whether the overrun occurs is very data dependent and in fact it is difficult to construct a test case by hand that triggers the bug. Second, the routine in question only reads past the end of the array (no memory locations are written), so it is quite likely that the program will succeed in spite of the error. This bug is synthetic (it never occurred in Moss) but is derived from bug #8.

8. This bug is a variant on bug #7, in another routine that deals with duplicates, but bug #8 occurs under an even rarer set of circumstances. In fact, this bug was never known to have caused a failure in Moss; it was discovered by a code review.

9. This bug is a variant of bug #4, but involves a different command-line argument and a different array.

In summary, the nine bugs are all either real bugs in Moss or bugs closely related to real bugs in Moss or other programs. The bugs range from typical C coding errors (e.g., NULL pointer dereferences and array overruns) to high-level violations of a system's internal invariants (e.g., bugs #1 and #3).

To allow us to measure the accuracy of our techniques we also added code to Moss to log when each bug was triggered. We were careful to exclude this code from the code that was instrumented for sampling, as predicates on the logging code would be very highly correlated with program failures.

To determine whether a run produced correct output we compare it against the output from a reference version of Moss without reintroduced bugs. As suggested in Sect. 1.4, in practice the labeling of runs as successful or failed might be done by detecting crashes, by noting internal assertion failures, or perhaps even by direct user feedback that the output of the program appears incorrect. Our use of a debugged reference version of Moss is merely an experimental convenience: an oracle that makes it possible for us to label large numbers of runs automatically.

4.4.1 Nonuniform Sampling

Sampling creates additional challenges that must be faced by any bug isolation algorithm. Assume that P_1 and P_2 behave identically in all possible runs, that both are sampled at a rate of $1/100$, and that both are reached once per run. Then even though P_1 and P_2 are equivalent, there is only a $1/100^2$ chance of both being observed to be true in a single run. These predicates will be observed in nearly disjoint sets of runs and can easily be misinterpreted as two distinct predictors for two distinct bugs rather than two equivalent predictors for a single bug.

To address this problem, we conducted the MOSS experiment with the sampling rates of instrumentation sites set in inverse proportion to their frequency of execution. Based on a training set of 1,000 executions, we set the sampling rate of each site so as to obtain an expected 100 samples of each site in subsequent program executions, but never below a minimum rate of $1/100$. Thus, rarely executed code has a much higher sampling rate than very frequently executed code. A similar strategy has been pursued for similar reasons in related work [12].

For reasons of experimental convenience, MOSS was actually run with complete data collection. Sampling was applied after the fact, as an offline postprocessing step. Section 2.4 discussed some implementation strategies for true, dynamically nonuniform sampling. For a controlled experiment, though, offline downsampling gave us greater freedom to experiment with different sampling options while holding the true, complete data fixed. We simulate incomplete data by sampling values from binomial distributions on the complete data with appropriate probabilities at each site. Because our runtime sampling is a Bernoulli process, the resulting data is exactly equivalent to that which would result from true sampling at runtime.

We also activated more instrumentation: the branches scheme, the returns scheme, and the scalar-pairs scheme with comparison to both variables and constants. These form a reasonably general starting set in the general case of a program whose number and kind of bugs are not already known. We generated 32,300 randomized runs and used them to construct a regularized logistic regression model.

4.4.2 Analysis Results

A weakness of logistic regression for our application is that it seeks to cover the set of failing runs without regard to the orthogonality of the selected predicates (i.e., whether they represent distinct bugs). This problem can be seen in Table 4.1, which gives the top ten predicates selected by logistic regression for our controlled MOSS experiment. The striking fact is that all selected predicates are either sub-bug or super-bug predictors. The predicates beginning with p + ... are all sub-bug predictors of bug #1 (see Table 4.6). The predicates i > ... are super-bug predictors: i is the length of the command line and the predicates say program crashes are more likely for long command lines (recall Sect. 4.3.4).

The prevalence of super-bug predictors on the list shows the difficulty of making use of the penalty term. Limiting the number of predicates that can be selected via a

Table 4.1. Results of regularized logistic regression for MOSS

β Coefficient	Predicate
0.769379	`(p + passage_index)->last_line < 4`
0.686149	`(p + passage_index)->first_line < i`
0.675982	`i > 20`
0.671991	`i > 26`
0.619479	`(p + passage_index)->last_line < i`
0.600712	`i > 23`
0.591044	`(p + passage_index)->last_line == next`
0.567753	`i > 22`
0.544829	`i > 25`
0.536122	`i > 28`

penalty has the effect of encouraging regularized logistic regression to choose super-bug predictors, as these cover more failing runs at the expense of poorer predictive power compared to predictors of individual bugs. On the other hand, the sub-bug predictors are chosen based on their excellent prediction power of those small subsets of failed runs. Relaxing the penalty allows logistic regression to add more predicates to improve its prediction, but then sub-bug predictors apparently are favored instead.

4.5 Iterative Bug Isolation and Elimination

Difficulties with logistic regression prompt us to consider a completely different analysis strategy based on filtering and iterative ranking of failure predictors. This algorithm can be seen as a generalization of the simpler elimination algorithm in Sect. 4.2. The idea is to simulate the iterative manner in which human programmers might find and fix bugs:

1. Identify the most important bug B.
2. Fix B, and repeat.

This section presents our algorithm for automatically isolating multiple bugs. As discussed in Sect. 4.1, the input is a set of feedback reports from individual program runs R, where $R(P) > 0$ if predicate P is observed to be true at least once during the execution of R.

For our purposes, identifying a bug B_i means selecting a predicate P_i closely correlated with a bug profile (subset of failing runs) $\mathcal{B}_i$. The difficulty is that we know the set of runs that succeed and fail, but we do not know which set of failing runs corresponds to B, or even how many bugs there are. In other words, we do not know the sizes or membership of the set of bug profiles. Thus, in the first step we must infer which predicates are most likely to correspond to individual bugs and rank those predicates in importance.

For the second step, while we cannot literally fix the bug corresponding to the chosen predictor P, we can simulate what happens if the bug does not occur. We discard any run R such that $R(P) > 0$ and repeat. Discarding all the runs where $R(P) > 0$ reduces the importance of other predictors of B, allowing predicates that predict different bugs (i.e., corresponding to different sets of failing runs) to rise to the top in subsequent iterations.

4.5.1 Increase Scores

We now discuss the first step: how to find the cause of the most important bug. We break this step into two sub-steps. First, we eliminate predicates that have no predictive power at all, which typically reduces the number of predicates we need to consider by two orders of magnitude (e.g., from hundreds of thousands to thousands). Next, we rank the surviving predicates by importance (see Sect. 4.5.3).

Consider the following C code fragment:

```
f = ...;                                               (a)
if (f == NULL) {                                       (b)
    x = 0;                                             (c)
    *f;                                                (d)
}
```

Consider the predicate f == NULL at line (b), which would be captured by branches instrumentation. Clearly this predicate is highly correlated with failure; in fact, whenever it is true this program inevitably crashes.[2] An important observation, however, is that there is no one perfect predictor of failure in a program with multiple bugs. Even a "smoking gun" such as f == NULL at line (b) has little or no predictive power for failures due to unrelated bugs in the same program.

The bug in the code fragment above is *deterministic* with respect to f == NULL: if f == NULL is true at line (b), the program fails. In many cases it is impossible to observe the exact conditions causing failure; for example, buffer overrun bugs in a C program may or may not cause the program to crash depending on runtime system decisions about how data is laid out in memory. Such bugs are *non-deterministic* with respect to every predicate; even for the best predictor P, it is possible that P is true and still the program terminates normally. In the example above, if we insert before line (d) a valid pointer assignment to f controlled by a conditional that is true at least occasionally (say via a call to read input)

```
if (...)
    f = ...some valid pointer ...;
*f;
```

then the bug becomes non-deterministic with respect to f == NULL.

To summarize, even for a predicate P that is truly the cause of a bug, we can neither assume that when P is true that the program fails nor that when P is never

---

[2] We also note that this bug could be detected by a simple static analysis; this example is meant to be concise rather than a significant application of our techniques.

observed to be true that the program succeeds. But we can express the probability that P being true implies failure. Let *Crash* be an atomic predicate that is true for failing runs and false for successful runs. Let $Pr(A|B)$ denote the conditional probability function of the event A given event B. We want to compute:

$$Fail(P) \equiv Pr(Crash|P \text{ observed to be true})$$

for every instrumented predicate P over the set of all runs. Let $S(P)$ be the number of successful runs in which P is observed to be true at least once, and let $F(P)$ be the number of failing runs in which P is observed to be true at least once. We estimate $Fail(P)$ as:

$$Fail(P) = \frac{F(P)}{S(P) + F(P)}$$

Notice that $Fail(P)$ is unaffected by the set of runs in which P is not observed to be true. Thus, if P is the cause of a bug, the causes of other independent bugs do not affect $Fail(P)$. Also note that runs in which P is not observed at all (either because the line of code on which P is checked is not reached, or the line is reached but P is not sampled) have no effect on $Fail(P)$. The definition of $Fail(P)$ generalizes the idea of deterministic and non-deterministic bugs. A bug is deterministic for P if $Fail(P) = 1.0$, or equivalently, P is never observed to be true in a successful run ($S(P) = 0$) and P is observed to be true in at least one failing run ($F(P) > 0$). If $Fail(P) < 1.0$ then the bug is non-deterministic with respect to P. Lower scores show weaker correlation between the predicate and program failure.

Now $Fail(P)$ is a useful measure, but it is not good enough for the first step of our algorithm. To see why, consider again the code fragment given above in its original, deterministic form. At line (b) we have $Fail(\text{f == NULL}) = 1.0$, so this predicate is a good candidate for the cause of the bug. But on line (c) we have the unpleasant fact that $Fail(\text{x == 0}) = 1.0$ as well. To understand why, observe that the predicate x == 0 is always true at line (c) and, in addition, only failing runs reach this line. Thus $S(\text{x == 0}) = 0$, and, so long as there is at least one run that reaches line (c) at all, $Fail(\text{x == 0})$ at line (c) is 1.0.

As this example shows, just because $Fail(P)$ is high does not mean P is the cause of a bug. In the case of x == 0, the decision that eventually causes the crash is made earlier, and the high $Fail(\text{x == 0})$ score merely reflects the fact that this predicate is checked on a path where the program is already doomed.

A way to address this difficulty is to score a predicate not by the chance that it implies failure, but by how much difference it makes that the predicate is observed to be true versus simply reaching the line where the predicate is checked. That is, on line (c), the probability of crashing is already 1.0 regardless of the value of the predicate x == 0, and thus the fact that x == 0 is true does not increase the probability of failure at all. This coincides with our intuition that this predicate is irrelevant to the bug.

Recall that we write "P observed" when P has been reached and sampled at least once, without regard to whether P was actually true or false. This convention leads us to the following definition:

$$Context(P) \equiv Pr(Crash|P \text{ observed})$$

Now, it is not the case that P is observed in every run, because the site where this predicate occurs may not be reached, or may be reached but not sampled. Thus, $Context(P)$ is the probability that in the subset of runs where the site containing predicate P is reached and sampled, the program fails. We can estimate $Context(P)$ as follows:

$$Context(P) = \frac{F(P \text{ observed})}{S(P \text{ observed}) + F(P \text{ observed})}$$

The interesting quantity, then, is

$$Increase(P) \equiv Fail(P) - Context(P)$$

which can be read as: How much does P being true increase the probability of failure over simply reaching the line where P is sampled? For example, for the predicate x == 0 on line (c), we have

$$Fail(\text{x == 0}) = Context(\text{x == 0}) = 1.0$$

and so $Increase(\text{x == 0}) = 0$.

A predicate P with $Increase(P) \leq 0$ has no predictive power. Being true does not increase the probability of failure, and we can safely discard all such predicates. But because some $Increase(P)$ scores may be based on few observations of P, it is important to attach confidence intervals to the scores. Since $Increase(P)$ is a statistic, computing a confidence interval for the underlying parameter is a well-understood problem. In our experiments we retain a predicate P only if the 95% confidence interval based on $Increase(P)$ lies strictly above zero; this practice removes predicates from consideration that have high increase scores but very low confidence because of few observations.

Pruning predicates based on $Increase(P)$ has several desirable properties. It is easy to prove that large classes of irrelevant predicates always have scores ≤ 0. For example, any predicate that is unreachable, that is a program invariant, or that is obviously control-dependent on a true cause is eliminated by this test. It is also worth pointing out that this test tends to localize bugs at a point where the condition that causes the bug first becomes true, rather than at the crash site. For example, in the code fragment given above, the bug is attributed to the success of the conditional branch test f == NULL on line (b) rather than the pointer dereference on line (d). Thus, the cause of the bug discovered by the algorithm points directly to the conditions under which the crash occurs, rather than the line on which it occurs (which is usually available anyway in the stack trace).

4.5.2 Statistical Interpretation

We have explained the test $Increase(P) > 0$ using programming terminology, but it also has a natural statistical interpretation as a simplified likelihood ratio hypothesis test. Consider the two classes of trial runs of the program: failed runs F and successful runs S. For each class, we can treat the predicate P as a Bernoulli random variable with heads probabilities $\pi_f(P)$ and $\pi_s(P)$, respectively, for the two classes. The heads probability is the probability that the predicate is observed to be true. If a predicate causes a set of crashes, then π_f should be much bigger than π_s. We can formulate two statistical hypotheses: the null hypothesis $\mathcal{H}_0 : \pi_f \leq \pi_s$, versus the alternate hypothesis $\mathcal{H}_1 : \pi_f > \pi_s$. Since π_f and π_s are not known, we must estimate them:

$$\hat{\pi}_f(P) = \frac{F(P)}{F(P \text{ observed})} \qquad\qquad \hat{\pi}_s(P) = \frac{S(P)}{S(P \text{ observed})}$$

Although these proportion estimates of π_f and π_s approach the actual heads probabilities as we increase the number of trial runs, they still differ due to sampling. With a certain probability, using these estimates instead of the actual values results in the wrong answer. A *likelihood ratio test* takes this uncertainty into account, and makes use of the statistic $Z = \frac{(\hat{\pi}_f - \hat{\pi}_s)}{V_{f,s}}$, where $V_{f,s}$ is a sample variance term (see, e.g., [38]). When the data size is large, Z can be approximated as a standard Gaussian random variable. Performed independently for each predicate P, the test decides whether or not $\pi_f(P) \leq \pi_s(P)$ with a guaranteed false-positive probability (i.e., choosing $\mathcal{H}_1$ when $\mathcal{H}_0$ is true). A necessary (but not sufficient) condition for choosing $\mathcal{H}_1$ is that $\hat{\pi}_f(P) > \hat{\pi}_s(P)$. However, this condition is equivalent to the condition that $Increase(P) > 0$. To see why, let $a = F(P)$, $b = S(P)$, $c = F(P \text{ observed})$, and $d = S(P \text{ observed})$. Then

$$Increase(P) > 0 \iff Fail(P) > Context(P)$$
$$\iff \frac{a}{a+b} > \frac{c}{c+d} \iff a(c+d) > (a+b)c$$
$$\iff ad > bc \iff \frac{a}{c} > \frac{b}{d} \iff \hat{\pi}_f(P) > \hat{\pi}_s(P)$$

4.5.3 Balancing Specificity and Sensitivity

We now turn to the question of ranking those predicates that survive pruning. Tables 4.2 through 4.4 show the top predicates under different ranking schemes (explained below) for one of our experiments. Additional per-predicate information, such as source file and line number, is available in an interactive version of our analysis tools.

We use a concise *bug thermometer* to visualize the information for each predicate. The length of the thermometer is logarithmic in the number of runs in which the predicate was observed, so small increases in thermometer size indicate many more runs. Each thermometer has a sequence of bands. The black band on the left shows $Context(P)$ as a fraction of the entire thermometer length. The dark gray band (▆) shows the lower bound of $Increase(P)$ with 95% confidence, also proportional to the entire thermometer length. The light gray band (▆) shows the size of that confidence interval. It is very small in most thermometers, indicating a tight interval. The white space at the right end of the thermometer shows $S(P)$, the number of successful runs in which the predicate was observed to be true. The tables show the thermometer as well as the numbers for each of the quantities that make up the thermometer.

The most important bug is the one that causes the greatest number of failed runs. This observation suggests:

$$Importance(P) = F(P)$$

Table 4.2 shows the top predicates ranked by decreasing $F(P)$ after predicates where $Increase(P) \leq 0$ are discarded. The predicates in Table 4.2 are, as expected, involved in many failing runs. However, the large white band in each thermometer reveals that these predicates are also highly non-deterministic: they are also true in many successful runs and are weakly correlated with bugs. Furthermore, the very narrow dark gray bands (■) in most thermometers indicate that most *Increase* scores are very small.

Our experience with other ranking strategies that emphasize the number of failed runs is similar. They select predicates involved in many failing, but also many successful, runs. The best of these predicates (the ones with high *Increase* scores) are super-bug predictors: predictors that include failures from more than one bug. Super-bug predictors account for a very large number of failures (by combining the failures of multiple bugs) but are also highly non-deterministic despite reasonably high *Increase* scores.

Another possibility is:

$$Importance(P) = Increase(P)$$

Table 4.3 shows the top predicates ranked by decreasing *Increase* score. Thermometers here are almost entirely dark gray (■), indicating *Increase* scores that are very close to 1.0. These predicates do a much better job of predicting failure. In fact, the program always fails when any of these predicates is true. However, observe that the number of failing runs (F) is very small. These predicates are *sub-bug predictors*: predictors for a subset of the failures caused by a bug. Unlike super-bug predictors, which are not useful in our experience, sub-bug predictors that account for a significant fraction of the failures for a bug often provide valuable clues. However, they still represent special cases and may mask other, more fundamental, causes of the bug.

Tables 4.2 and 4.3 illustrate the difficulty of defining "importance." We are looking for predicates with high *sensitivity*, meaning predicates that account for many failed runs. But we also want high *specificity*, meaning predicates that do not mispredict failure in many successful runs. In information retrieval, the corresponding terms are *recall* and *precision*. A standard way to combine sensitivity and specificity is to compute their harmonic mean; this measure prefers high scores in both dimensions. In our case, $Increase(P)$ measures specificity. For sensitivity, we have found it useful to consider a transformation ϕ of the raw counts, and to form the normalized ratio $\phi(F(P))/\phi(NumF)$, where $NumF$ is the total number of failed runs. In our work thus far ϕ has been a logarithmic transformation, which moderates the impact of very large numbers of failures. Thus our overall metric is the following:

Table 4.2. Moss failure predictors sorted by F(P)

Thermometer	Context	Increase	S|	F	F+S	Predicate
	0.176	0.007±0.012	22554	5045	27599	files[filesindex].language != 15
	0.176	0.007±0.012	22566	5045	27611	tmp == 0 is FALSE
	0.176	0.007±0.012	22571	5045	27616	strcmp != 0
	0.176	0.007±0.013	18894	4251	23145	tmp == 0 is FALSE
	0.176	0.007±0.013	18885	4240	23125	files[filesindex].language != 14
	0.177	0.008±0.013	17757	4007	21764	filesindex >= 25
	0.176	0.008±0.014	16453	3731	20184	M < M
	0.177	0.261±0.023	4800	3716	8516	config.winnowing_window_size != argc
	0.131	0.012±0.014	15325	3567	18892	i > 21
	0.176	0.018±0.012	17846	3125	20971	token_sequence[token_index].lineno <= token_index
	0.176	0.077±0.018	9136	3104	12240	tmp == 0 is FALSE
	0.131	0.077±0.018	9126	3095	12221	files[filesindex].language >= 14
	0.129	0.021±0.013	17256	3092	20348	token_index > lineno
	0.131	0.021±0.012	17589	3084	20673	i >= lineno
	0.176	0.023±0.013	16895	3060	19955	token_sequence[token_index].lineno < token_index
	0.115	0.020±0.015	12550	3056	15606	filesIndex > 30
	0.176	0.008±0.011	21431	2985	24416	passage_index > yy_start
	0.112	0.021±0.016	11967	2935	14902	i > 24
	0.110	0.007±0.011	21403	2894	24297	min_index > yy_start
	0.135	0.007±0.011	21322	2826	24148	min_index > yy_start
	0.176	0.021±0.013	14493	2677	17170	fin_> fin
	0.176	0.199±0.024	4332	2595	6927	config.winnowing_window_size < argc
	0.176	0.398±0.030	1924	2592	4516	i >= 8
	0.176	0.398±0.030	1924	2592	4516	i >= 6
	0.176	0.398±0.030	1924	2592	4516	i >= 2
	0.176	0.398±0.030	1924	2592	4516	i >= 4
	0.107	0.010±0.011	19385	2585	21970	(p + passage_index)->last_line <= filesindex
	0.107	0.006±0.011	20119	2578	22697	(p + passage_index)->last_line < last
	0.114	0.011±0.012	18046	2577	20623	(p + passage_index)->last_line <= filesindex
	0.107	0.011±0.011	19081	2568	21649	(p + passage_index)->last_line < filesindex
	0.129	0.007±0.011	19975	2568	22543	(p + passage_index)->first_line < fileid
	0.114	0.010±0.013	15906	2556	18462	i > 28
	0.116	0.012±0.012	17613	2551	20164	(p + passage_index)->last_line < filesindex
	0.116	0.027±0.013	15100	2517	17617	i > lineno
	0.114	0.025±0.013	15175	2506	17681	start > lineno
	0.115	0.008±0.012	17862	2491	20353	(p + passage_index)->first_line < fileid
	0.107	0.009±0.012	17554	2480	20034	(p + passage_index)->first_line < last
	0.107	0.064±0.014	11962	2464	14426	(p + passage_index)->first_line <= i

2701 additional predictors follow ....

Table 4.3. Moss failure predictors sorted by Increase(P)

Thermometer	Context	Increase	S	F	F + S	Predicate
	0.065	0.935±0.019	0	23	23	((*(fi + i)))->this.last_token < filesbase
	0.065	0.935±0.020	0	10	10	((*(fi + i)))->other.last_line == last
	0.071	0.929±0.020	0	18	18	((*(fi + i)))->other.last_line == filesbase
	0.073	0.927±0.020	0	10	10	((*(fi + i)))->other.last_line == yy_n_chars
	0.071	0.929±0.028	0	19	19	bytes <= filesbase
	0.075	0.925±0.022	0	14	14	((*(fi + i)))->other.first_line == 2
	0.076	0.924±0.022	0	12	12	((*(fi + i)))->this.first_line < nid
	0.077	0.923±0.023	0	10	10	((*(fi + i)))->other.last_line == yy_init
	0.080	0.920±0.023	0	10	10	((*(fi + i)))->other.last_line == yy_n_chars
	0.080	0.920±0.023	0	12	12	((*(fi + i)))->other.last_line == numlines_other
	0.081	0.919±0.023	0	12	12	((*(fi + i)))->this.last_line == lineno
	0.082	0.918±0.024	0	10	10	((*(fi + i)))->this.last_line <= yy_start
	0.082	0.918±0.024	0	11	11	((*(fi + i)))->this.last_line == htmlscope
	0.085	0.915±0.023	0	11	11	((*(fi + i)))->this.first_line < 7
	0.085	0.915±0.024	0	10	10	((*(fi + i)))->other.last_line == lineno
	0.087	0.913±0.025	0	12	12	((*(fi + i)))->other.last_line < yy_start
	0.087	0.913±0.024	0	14	14	((*(fi + i)))->other.first_line < 3
	0.091	0.909±0.025	0	10	10	((*(fi + i)))->this.last_line <= 1
	0.100	0.900±0.009	0	526	526	yy_start == 17
	0.100	0.900±0.009	0	503	503	yy_start > 16
	0.101	0.899±0.009	0	522	522	yy_start > 11
	0.114	0.886±0.007	0	66	66	last > 500
	0.115	0.885±0.007	0	67	67	first > 500
	0.117	0.883±0.011	1	79	79	((*(fi + i)))->other.last_token <= filesbase
	0.116	0.883±0.012	1	769	770	((*(fi + i)))->other.last_line == yy_start
	0.118	0.882±0.011	0	22	22	((*(fi + i)))->this.last_token == filesbase
	0.116	0.883±0.012	1	774	775	((*(fi + i)))->this.last_line == 1
	0.116	0.883±0.011	0	776	777	((*(fi + i)))->other.last_line == yyleng
	0.118	0.882±0.011	0	13	13	((*(fi + i)))->other.last_line > pindex
	0.118	0.881±0.012	1	769	770	((*(fi + i)))->this.last_line < 2
	0.118	0.881±0.012	1	771	772	((*(fi + i)))->this.last_line == yy_start
	0.118	0.881±0.012	1	773	773	((*(fi + i)))->other.last_line == 1
	0.118	0.880±0.012	1	776	777	((*(fi + i)))->other.last_line < 2
	0.118	0.880±0.013	2	772	774	((*(fi + i)))->this.last_line == yyleng
	0.124	0.876±0.008	0	384	384	config.language == 17
	0.124	0.876±0.008	0	391	391	config.language > 16
	0.117	0.876±0.016	6	781	787	((*(fi + i)))->this.last_line == diff
	0.116	0.875±0.017	7	784	791	((*(fi + i)))->other.last_line == diff
	0.131	0.869±0.008	0	633	633	files[fileid].size < token_index

2701 additional predictors follow . . . .

$$Importance(P) = \frac{2}{\frac{1}{Increase(P)} + \frac{1}{log(F(P))/log(NumF)}}$$

Table 4.4 gives results using this metric. Individual $F(P)$ counts are smaller than in Table 4.2, and individual $Increase(P)$ scores are smaller than in Table 4.3, but the harmonic mean has effectively balanced both of these important factors. All of the predicates on this list indeed have both high specificity and sensitivity. Each of these predictors accurately describes a large number of failures.

4.5.4 Redundancy Elimination

The remaining problem with the results in Table 4.4 is that there is substantial redundancy; it is easy to see that several of these predicates are related. This redundancy hides other, distinct bugs that either have fewer failed runs or more non-deterministic predictors further down the list. As discussed above, we use a simple iterative algorithm to eliminate redundant predicates:

1. Rank predicates by *Importance*.
2. Remove the top-ranked predicate P and discard all runs R (feedback reports) where $R(P) > 0$.
3. Repeat these steps until the set of runs is empty or the set of predicates is empty.

We can now state an easy-to-prove but important property of this algorithm.

Lemma 1. *Let $P_1, \ldots, P_n$ be a set of instrumented predicates, $B_1, \ldots, B_m$ a set of bugs, and $\mathcal{B}_1, \ldots, \mathcal{B}_m$ the corresponding bug profiles. Let*

$$\mathcal{Z} = \bigcup_{1 \leq i \leq n} \{R | R(P_i) > 0\}.$$

If for all $1 \leq j \leq m$ we have $\mathcal{B}_j \cap \mathcal{Z} \neq \emptyset$, then the algorithm chooses at least one predicate from the list $P_1, \ldots, P_n$ that predicts at least one failure due to B_j.

Thus, the elimination algorithm chooses at least one predicate predictive of each bug represented by the input set of predicates. We are, in effect, covering the set of bugs with a ranked subset of predicates. The other property we might like, that the algorithm chooses exactly one predicate to represent each bug, does not hold; we shall see in Sect. 4.6 that the algorithm sometimes selects a strong sub-bug predictor as well as a more natural predictor.

Beyond always representing each bug, the algorithm works well for two other reasons. First, two predicates are redundant if they predict the same (or nearly the same) set of failing runs. Thus, simply removing the set of runs in which a predicate is true automatically dramatically reduces the importance of any related predicates in the correct proportions. Second, because elimination is iterative, it is only necessary that *Importance* selects a good predictor at each step, and not necessarily the best one; any predicate that covers a different set of failing runs than all higher-ranked predicates is selected eventually.

Table 4.4. MOSS failure predictors sorted by harmonic mean

Thermometer	Context	Increase	$	F	F + S	Predicate
	0.176	0.824±0.009	0	1585	1585	files[filesindex].language > 16
	0.176	0.824±0.009	0	1584	1584	strcmp > 0
	0.176	0.824±0.009	0	1580	1580	strcmp == 0
	0.176	0.824±0.009	0	1577	1577	files[filesindex].language == 17
	0.176	0.824±0.009	0	1576	1576	tmp == 0 is TRUE
	0.176	0.824±0.009	0	1573	1573	strcmp > 0
	0.116	0.883±0.012	1	774	775	(*(fi + i)))->this.last_line == 1
	0.116	0.883±0.012	1	776	777	(*(fi + i)))->other.last_line == yyleng
	0.111	0.832±0.027	73	1203	1276	config.match_comment is TRUE
	0.118	0.880±0.012	1	769	770	(*(fi + i)))->other.last_line == yy_start
	0.118	0.881±0.012	1	776	777	(*(fi + i)))->other.last_line < 2
	0.118	0.881±0.012	1	771	773	(*(fi + i)))->other.last_line == 1
	0.118	0.881±0.012	1	769	772	(*(fi + i)))->this.last_line == yy_start
	0.118	0.880±0.013	2	772	774	(*(fi + i)))->this.last_line < 2
	0.117	0.876±0.016	6	781	787	(*(fi + i)))->this.last_line == yyleng
	0.116	0.875±0.017	7	784	791	(*(fi + i)))->this.last_line == diff
	0.115	0.866±0.021	16	826	842	(*(fi + i)))->other.last_line == diff
	0.117	0.855±0.024	25	864	889	(*(fi + i)))->other.last_line <= 3
	0.131	0.810±0.026	79	1258	1337	token_sequence[token_index].val >= 100
	0.118	0.863±0.021	15	798	813	(*(fi + i)))->other.last_line <= 2
	0.116	0.865±0.021	14	787	801	(*(fi + i)))->this.last_line <= 2
	0.118	0.851±0.026	30	862	892	(*(fi + i)))->other.last_line <= 4
	0.131	0.855±0.025	22	776	798	(*(fi + i)))->this.last_line == nextstate
	0.131	0.859±0.016	7	711	718	token_index > 500
	0.119	0.869±0.008	0	639	639	files[fileid].size < token_count
	0.131	0.849±0.027	26	779	805	(*(fi + i)))->other.last_line == nextstate
	0.100	0.869±0.008	0	633	633	files[fileid].size < token_index
	0.100	0.900±0.009	0	526	526	yy_start == 17
	0.101	0.899±0.009	0	522	522	yy_start > 11
	0.117	0.844±0.028	32	794	826	config.match_comment is TRUE
	0.118	0.829±0.031	49	876	925	(*(fi + i)))->this.last_line < nid
	0.115	0.796±0.032	115	1171	1286	(p + passage_index)->last_line < 2
	0.100	0.900±0.009	0	503	503	yy_start > 16
	0.117	0.828±0.031	52	879	931	(*(fi + i)))->other.last_line < nid
	0.116	0.839±0.030	37	794	831	(*(fi + i)))->other.last_line <= diff
	0.117	0.840±0.030	36	788	824	(*(fi + i)))->this.last_line <= diff
	0.116	0.818±0.033	65	914	979	(*(fi + i)))->this.last_line < 8
	0.118	0.833±0.031	40	778	818	(*(fi + i)))->this.last_line <= nextstate

2701 additional predictors follow

Table 4.5. Summary statistics for bug isolation experiments

		Runs			Predicate Counts		
	Line Count	Successful	Failing	Sites	Initial	*Increase* > 0	Elimination
MOSS	6,001	26,299	5,598	35,223	202,998	2,740	21
CCRYPT	5,276	20,684	10,316	9,948	58,720	50	2
BC	14,288	23,198	7,802	50,171	298,482	147	2
RHYTHMBOX	56,484	12,530	19,431	145,176	857,384	537	15
EXIF	10,588	30,789	2,211	27,380	156,476	272	3

4.6 Case Studies

In this section we present the results of applying the algorithm described in Sect. 4.5 in five case studies. Complete analysis results for all experiments in this section may be browsed interactively at <http://www.cs.wisc.edu/~liblit/dissertation/supplemental/> or on an archival DVD accompanying the original dissertation.

Table 4.5 shows summary statistics for each of the experiments. In each study we ran the programs on about 32,000 random inputs. The number of instrumentation sites varies with the size of the program, as does the number of predicates those instrumentation sites yield. Our algorithm is very effective in reducing the number of predicates the user must examine. For example, in the case of RHYTHMBOX an initial set of 857,384 predicates is reduced to 537 by the $Increase(P) > 0$ test, a reduction of 99.9%. The elimination algorithm then yields 15 predicates, a further reduction of 97%. The other case studies show a similar reduction in the number of predicates by 3-4 orders of magnitude.

All results that follow are derived from sampled data collected as in Sect. 4.4.1: nonuniform sampling, inversely linear in site coverage based on 1,000 training runs, set to yield an expected 100 samples per site, with a minimum rate of $1/100$. We have validated this approach by comparing the results for each experiment with results obtained with no sampling at all (i.e., the sampling rate of all predicates set to 100%). The results are identical except for the RHYTHMBOX and MOSS experiments, where we judge the differences to be minor: sometimes a different but logically equivalent predicate is chosen, the ranking of predictors of different bugs is slightly different, or one or the other version has a few extra, weak predictors at the tail end of the list.

4.6.1 MOSS

We begin by applying the elimination algorithm to MOSS, using the same seeded bugs and the same initial feedback data that stumped regularized logistic regression in Sect. 4.4. Table 4.6 shows the results of the elimination algorithm on the same data. The predicates listed were selected by the elimination algorithm in the order shown. The first column is the initial bug thermometer for each predicate, showing the *Context* and *Increase* scores before elimination is performed. The fourth column is the *effective* bug thermometer, showing the *Context* and *Increase* scores for a predicate P at the time P is selected (i.e., when it is the top-ranked predicate). Thus the

Table 4.6. Moss failure predictors using nonuniform sampling

Initial	Effective	Predicate	Number of Runs Also Exhibiting Bug #n							
			#1	#2	#3	#4	#5	#6	#7	#9
		files[filesindex].language > 16	0	0	28	54	1585	0	0	68
		((*(fi + i)))->this.last_line == 1	774	0	17	0	0	0	18	2
		token_index > 500	31	0	16	711	0	0	0	47
		(p + passage_index)->last_token <= filesbase	28	2	508	0	0	0	1	29
		result == 0 is TRUE	16	0	0	9	19	291	0	13
		config.match_comment is TRUE	791	2	23	1	0	5	11	41
		i == yy_last_accepting_state	55	0	21	0	0	3	7	769
		f < f	3	144	2	2	0	0	0	5
		files[fileid].size < token_index	31	0	10	633	0	0	0	40
		passage_index == 293	27	3	8	0	0	0	2	366
		((*(fi + i)))->other.last_line == yyleng	776	0	16	0	0	0	18	1
		min_index == 64	24	1	7	0	0	1	1	249
		((*(fi + i)))->this.last_line == yy_start	771	0	18	0	0	0	19	0
		(passages + i)->fileid == 52	24	0	477	14	24	0	1	14
		passage_index == 25	60	5	27	0	0	4	10	962
		strcmp > 0	0	0	28	54	1584	0	0	68
		i > 500	32	2	18	853	54	0	0	53
		token_sequence[token_index].val >= 100	1250	3	28	38	0	15	19	65
		i == 50	27	0	11	0	0	1	4	463
		passage_index == 19	59	5	28	0	0	4	10	958
		bytes <= filesbase	1	0	19	0	0	0	0	1

effective thermometer reflects the cumulative diluting effect of redundancy elimination for all predicates selected before this one.

As part of the experiment we separately recorded the exact set of bugs that actually occurred in each run. The columns at the far right of Table 4.6 show, for each selected predicate and for each bug, the number of runs in which both the selected predicate is observed to be true and the bug occurs. Note that while each predicate has a very strong spike at one bug, indicating it is a strong predictor of that bug, there are always some runs with other bugs present. For example, the top-ranked predicate, which is overwhelmingly a predictor of bug #5, also includes some runs where bugs #3, #4, and #9 occurred. This situation is not the result of misclassification of failing runs by our algorithm. Rather, more than one bug may occur in a run. It simply happens that in some runs bugs #5 and #3 both occur (to pick just one possible combination).

A particularly interesting case of this phenomenon is bug #7, one of the buffer overruns. Bug #7 is not strongly predicted by any predicate on the list but in fact occurs in at least a few of the failing runs of most predicates. We have examined the runs of bug #7 in detail and found that the bug #7 only occurs in runs that also trigger at least one other bug. That is, even when the bug #7 overrun happens, it never causes incorrect output or a crash in any run. Bug #8, another overrun, is not even shown because the overrun is never triggered in our data (its column would be all zeros). There is no way our algorithm can find causes of bugs that do not occur, but recall that part of our purpose in sampling user executions is to get an accurate picture of the most important bugs. It is consistent with this goal that if a bug never causes a problem, it is not only not worth fixing, it is not even worth reporting.

The other bugs all have strong predictors on the list. In fact, the top eight predicates have exactly one predictor for each of the seven bugs that occur, with the exception of bug #1, which has one very strong sub-bug predictor in the second spot and another predictor in the sixth position. Notice that even the rarest bug, bug #2, which occurs more than an order of magnitude less frequently than the most common bug, is identified immediately after the last of the other bugs.[3] Furthermore, we have verified by hand that the selected predicates would, in our judgment, lead an engineer to the cause of the bug. Overall, the elimination algorithm does an excellent job of listing separate causes of each of the bugs in order of priority, with very little redundancy.

Below the eighth position there are no new bugs to report and every predicate is correlated with predicates higher on the list. Even without the columns of numbers at the right it is easy to spot the eighth position as the natural cutoff. Keep in mind that the length of the thermometer is on a log scale, hence changes in larger magnitudes may appear less evident. Notice that the initial and effective thermometers for the first eight predicates are essentially identical. Only the predicate at position six is noticeably different, indicating that this predicate is somewhat affected by a predicate listed earlier (specifically, its companion sub-bug predictor at position two). However, all

---

[3] The peculiar eighth predicate, $f < f$, says that after an assignment the new value of f is less than the old value of f.

Table 4.7. Predictors for CCRYPT

Initial	Effective	Predicate
		res == nl
		line <= outfile

Table 4.8. Predictors for BC

Initial	Effective	Predicate
		a_names < v_names
		old_count == 32

of the predicates below the eighth line have very different initial and effective thermometers (either many fewer failing runs, or much more non-deterministic, or both) showing that these predicates are strongly affected by higher-ranked predicates.

The displays presented thus far have a drawback illustrated by the MOSS experiment: It is not easy to identify the predicates to which a predicate is closely related. Such a feature would be useful in confirming whether two selected predicates represent different bugs or are in fact related to the same bug. We do have a measure of how strongly P implies another predicate P': How does removing the runs where $R(P) > 0$ affect the importance of P'? The more closely related P and P' are, the more P''s importance drops when P's failing runs are removed. In the interactive version of our analysis tools, each predicate P in the final, ranked list of predicates can zoom in to a linked *affinity list* of all predicates ranked by how much P causes their ranking score to decrease.

4.6.2 CCRYPT

We revisited CCRYPT 1.2, which has a known input validation bug as discussed in Sect. 4.2.1. The results are shown in Table 4.7. Our algorithm reports two predictors, both of which point directly to the single bug. It is easy to discover that the two predictors are for the same bug; the first predicate is listed first in the second predicate's affinity list, indicating the first predicate is a sub-bug predictor associated with the second predicate.

4.6.3 BC

We revisited GNU BC 1.06, which has a buffer overrun bug as discussed in Sect. 4.3. Our results are shown in Table 4.8. The outcome is the same as for CCRYPT: two predicates are retained by elimination, and the second predicate lists the first predicate at the top of its affinity list, indicating that the first predicate is a sub-bug predictor of the second. Both predicates point to the cause of the overrun. This bug causes

Table 4.9. Predictors for EXIF

Initial	Effective	Predicate
		`i < 0`
		`maxlen > 1900`
		`o + s > buf_size is TRUE`

a crash long after the overrun occurs and there is no useful information on the stack at the point of the crash to assist in isolating this bug.

4.6.4 EXIF

Table 4.9 shows results for EXIF 0.6.9, an open source image processing program. Each of the three predicates is a predictor of a distinct and previously unknown crashing bug. It took less than 20 minutes of work to find and verify the cause of each of the bugs using these predicates and the additional highly correlated predicates on their affinity lists.

To illustrate how statistical debugging is used in practice, we use the last of these three failure predictors as an example, and describe how it guided us to the cause of one of the bugs. Failed runs exhibiting `o + s > buf_size` show the following unique stack trace at the point of termination:

```
main
    exif_data_save_data
        exif_data_save_data_content
            exif_data_save_data_content
                exif_data_save_data_entry
                    exif_mnote_data_save
                        exif_mnote_data_canon_save
                            memcpy
```

The code in the vicinity of this crash site is as follows:

```
// snippet of exif_mnote_data_canon_save
for (i = 0; i < n->count; i++) {
    ...
    memcpy(*buf + doff, n->entries[i].data, s);                  (c)
    ...
}
```

This stack trace alone provides little insight into the cause of the bug. However, our statistical debugging algorithm highlights `o + s > buf_size` in function `exif_mnote_data_canon_load` as a strong bug predictor. Thus, a quick inspection of the source code leads us to construct the following call sequence:

```
main
    exif_loader_get_data
        exif_data_load_data
            exif_mnote_data_canon_load
    exif_data_save_data
        exif_data_save_data_content
            exif_data_save_data_content
                exif_data_save_data_entry
                    exif_mnote_data_save
                        exif_mnote_data_canon_save
                            memcpy
```

The code in the vicinity of the predicate o + s > buf_size is as follows:

```
// snippet of exif_mnote_data_canon_load
for (i = 0; i < c; i++) {
    ...
    n->count = i + 1;
    ...
    if (o + s > buf_size) return;                          (a)
    ...
    n->entries[i].data = malloc(s);                        (b)
    ...
}
```

It is apparent from the above code snippets and the call sequence that whenever the predicate o + s > buf_size is true,

- the function exif_mnote_data_canon_load returns on line (a), skipping the call to malloc on line (b) and therefore leaving n->entries[i]->data uninitialized for some value of i, and
- the function exif_mnote_data_canon_save passes this uninitialized value from n->entries[i]->data to memcpy on line (c), which reads it and eventually crashes.

In summary, our algorithm enabled us to effectively isolate the causes of several previously unknown bugs in source code unfamiliar to us in a small amount of time and without any explicit specification beyond "the program shouldn't crash."

4.6.5 RHYTHMBOX

Table 4.10 shows our results for RHYTHMBOX 0.6.5, an interactive, graphical, open source music player. RHYTHMBOX is a complex, multi-threaded, event-driven system, written using a library providing object-oriented primitives in C. Event-driven systems use event queues; each event performs some computation and possibly adds more events to some queues. We know of no static analysis today that can analyze event-driven systems accurately, because no static analysis is currently capable of

Table 4.10. Predictors for RHYTHMBOX

Initial	Effective	Predicate
		`tmp is FALSE`
		`(mp->priv)->timer is FALSE`
		`(view->priv)->change_sig_queued is TRUE`
		`(hist->priv)->db is TRUE`
		`rb_playlist_manager_signals[0] > 269`
		`(db->priv)->thread_reaper_id >= 12`
		`entry == entry`
		`fn == fn`
		`klass > klass`
		`genre < artist`
		`vol <= (float )0 is TRUE`
		`(player->priv)->handling_error is TRUE`
		`(statusbar->priv)->library_busy is TRUE`
		`shell < shell`
		`len < 270`

analyzing the heap-allocated event queues with sufficient precision. Crash reporting systems are also of limited utility in analyzing event-driven systems, as the stack in the main event loop is unchanging and all of the interesting state is in the queues.

We isolated two distinct bugs in RHYTHMBOX. The first predicate in Table 4.10 led us to the discovery of a race condition. This bug turned out to be a previously unrecognized incorrect pattern of accessing the underlying object library. A simple syntactic static analysis subsequently showed more than one hundred instances of the same unsafe pattern throughout RHYTHMBOX. Perhaps the greatest strength of our system is its ability to automatically identify the cause of many different kinds of bugs, including new classes of bugs that we did not anticipate in building the tool. By relying only on the distinction between good and bad executions, our analysis does not require a specification of the program properties to be analyzed. Thus, statistical debugging provides a complementary approach to static analyses, which generally do require specification of the properties to check. Statistical debugging can identify bugs beyond the reach of static analysis techniques and even new classes of bugs that may be amenable to static analysis if anyone thought to check for them.

The second predicate from Table 4.10 was not useful directly, but we were able to isolate the bug using the predicates in its affinity list. In particular, the following strongly correlated predicate appears near the very top of that affinity list:

```
lib/disclosure-widget.c:77: in function cddb_source_destroy:
g_source_remove return value > 0
```

This related predicate is a true "smoking gun" that directly led us to both the problem and its solution. It tells us that RHYTHMBOX tends to fail when a particular call to g_source_remove returns a positive value. Library documentation [23] reveals that g_source_remove uses its integer return value as a success/failure code, as is common in C. Surprisingly, positive return values indicate *success*. This function call usually fails. In the rare case where the call succeeds, the entire program subsequently crashes. Of course this phenomenon is exactly the opposite of how we expected the returns instrumentation scheme to expose bugs, but it is just as effective. A simple syntactic static analysis revealed a second instance of the same bad code pattern. This second instance was ultimately found to be the cause of an open, previously reported RHYTHMBOX bug. That bug had gone undiagnosed and unfixed for several months due in part to the difficulty of reproducing the problem in a controlled test environment.

RHYTHMBOX developers confirmed the problems we found and enthusiastically applied patches within a few days, in part because we could quantify the bugs as important crashing bugs. It required several hours to isolate each of the two bugs, partly because RHYTHMBOX is complex and partly because the bugs were violations of subtle heap invariants that are not directly captured by our current instrumentation schemes. Note, however, that we could not have even begun to understand these bugs without the information provided by our tool. Exploring schemes that track predicates on heap structure remains an important area for future work.

5

Related Work

Given enough eyes, all bugs are shallow.

–Eric S. Raymond, The Cathedral and the Bazaar

Here we discuss a cross section of related work, loosely organized into three broad topics. We briefly visit static analyses that examine code without running it. We consider earlier approaches to profiling and tracing running code, most of which have concentrated on performance profiling. Lastly we review dynamic analyses that focus more directly on the problem of debugging, including several that use statistical methods.

5.1 Static Analysis

There is currently a great deal of interest in applying specialized static analysis to improve software quality. Static analyses can help to find bugs earlier in development when they are cheaper to fix. Purely analytic approaches build upon such formalisms as type systems [25, 37], automated theorem proving [22], and software model checking [31]. Some static analyses can guarantee that certain classes of bugs can never occur in any run. Strong assurances of this form may be required in certain domains, and cannot generally be obtained from dynamic schemes such as CBI.

While we firmly believe in the use of static analysis to find and prevent bugs, our dynamic approach has advantages as well. A dynamic analysis can observe actual run-time values, which is often better than either making a very conservative static assumption about run-time values for the sake of soundness, or allowing some very simple bugs to escape undetected. Another advantage of dynamic analysis, especially one that mines actual user executions for its data, is the ability to assign an accurate importance to each bug. Additionally, as we have shown, a dynamic analysis that does not require an explicit specification of the properties to check can find clues to a very wide range of errors, including classes of errors not considered in the design of the analysis.

A complementary family of static bug hunting tools places more emphasis on human factors in software development. Static metrics of software complexity and other factors can guide engineers to likely hiding places for bugs [51]. The chronological record captured by a source code control system can be mined to reveal areas

B. Liblit: Cooperative Bug Isolation, LNCS 4440, pp. 89–93, 2007.

of high code churn or to raise warning flags when code is changed in a manner inconsistent with historical patterns [63, 66]. Any of these systems might reasonably be integrated with Cooperative Bug Isolation, such as by increasing the sampling density in code that appears suspect.

5.2 Profiling and Tracing

Dynamic program sampling has a long history, with most applications focusing on performance profiling and optimization. Any sampling system must define a trigger mechanism that signals when a sample is to be taken. Typical triggers include periodic hardware timers or interrupts [9, 59, 61], periodic software event counters (e.g., every nth function call) [3], or a hardware/software mix. In most cases, the sampling interval is strictly periodic. Periodic sampling may suffice when hunting for large performance bottlenecks, but may systematically miss rare events.

The Digital Continuous Profiling Infrastructure [1] is unusual in choosing sampling intervals randomly. However, the random distribution is uniform, such as one sample every 60K to 64K cycles. Samples thus extracted are not independent. If one sample is taken, there is zero chance of taking any sample in the next 1–59,999 cycles and zero chance of *not* taking exactly one sample in the next 60K–64K cycles. We trigger samples based on a geometric distribution, which correctly models the interval between successful independent coin tosses. The resulting data is a statistically rigorous fair random sample, which in turn grants access to a large domain of powerful statistical analyses.

Recent work in trace collection has focused on program understanding. Techniques for capturing program traces confront challenges similar to those we face here, such as minimizing performance overhead and managing large quantities of captured data. Dynamic analysis in particular must encode, compress, or otherwise reduce an incoming trace stream in real time, as the program runs [14, 55]. It may be difficult to directly adapt dynamic trace analysis techniques to a domain where the trace is sampled and therefore incomplete.

Path profiling subsumes basic block and edge profiling to directly monitor how often each acyclic path in a program executes. Optimizations first developed by Ball and Larus [4] limit instrumentation to loop back edges and chord edges not in a special spanning tree constructed for each acyclic region. This work relates to ours in three respects. First, feedback reports containing path profiles may be an interesting target for bug isolation data mining. A program may succeed on most paths but fail on some others. Second, the acyclic regions we use for overhead amortization (Sect. 2.1.1) correspond well to those used by Ball and Larus to build spanning trees. It should not be difficult to integrate the two analyses, thereby collecting fair random samples of complete path profiles. Lastly, a variant of our proposed path balancing algorithm (Sect. 2.3.6) might be layered atop a path profiler. Paths within an acyclic region carry unique indexes. Instead of balancing all paths, a path-indexed table could record the exact (unbalanced) instrumentation weight for each path. This table would then be used to find the aggregated net decrement to the global next sample countdown for each uninstrumented traversal.

Subsection 2.1.2 discussed Arnold and Ryder's framework for lightweight instrumentation [2] and our adaptation of it to use strictly fair random sampling. Recent developments by Chilimbi and others adapt Arnold and Ryder's work in complementary ways. Hirzel and Chilimbi [32] collect temporal profile "bursts" by allowing execution to remain on the instrumented slow path for longer periods of time. This technique could augment our own, which currently provides only rudimentary temporal information in the form of time stamps (Sect. 2.2.3). Chilimbi and Hauswirth [12] adjust acyclic regions' sampling rates dynamically, within a single execution. This sort of rapid adjustment is useful when bench testing with few test cases. It may be less important when the "test cases" are users numbering in the thousands or millions. Performance overhead is quite small in both studies: 3-18% for the former and 3-6% for the later. We attribute this result to two factors. First, the sampling strategy is not truly statistically fair or random as in our work. This short cut eliminates some overhead, and in particular means that the fast path is completely instrumentation free. Our proposed path balancing algorithm (Sect. 2.3.6) also yields an instrumentation free fast path, and therefore may allow us to approach the same low overheads achieved by Chilimbi. Second, Chilimbi's implementation uses a binary rewriting system [16] rather than operating on source code. While we have found source-to-source transformation to be convenient for research, it does leave our performance subject to the whims of the native C compiler's optimizer. Direct binary manipulation may yield more reliable results.

5.3 Dynamic Analysis

Our effort to understand and debug programs by selecting predicates is partly inspired by Daikon [20]. Like Daikon, we begin with fairly unstructured guesses and eliminate those that do not appear to hold. Unlike Daikon, we are concerned with gathering data from production code, which leads us to use sampling of a large number of runs and statistical models; the Daikon experiments are done on a smaller number of complete traces. We are also interested in detecting bugs, while Daikon focuses on the somewhat different problem of detecting program invariants. Some initial efforts have been made to find bugs by comparing Daikon-detected invariants in good and bad runs [54]. This work is similar to our basic predicate elimination strategy of Sect. 4.2.

In a related project, Dodoo et al. [15] use clustering analysis to select conditional predicates of the form $p \implies q$ that might be true and that are worth tracking dynamically using Daikon. Our instrumentation schemes are currently quite simpleminded in how they select what might be interesting. Performance could certainly be improved by using static analysis to make more selective instrumentation choices up front. However, one must exercise caution: the formal semantics of buggy programs are rarely specified [62] and difficult to codify, especially if memory safety is not assured.

The DIDUCE project [27] also attempts to identify bugs using analysis of executions. Unlike Daikon, most processing does take place within the client program. As in our study, DIDUCE attempts to relate changes in predicates to the manifestation of bugs. However, DIDUCE performs complete tracing and focuses on discrete state changes, such as the first time a predicate transitioned from true to false. Our approach is more probabilistic: we wish to identify broad trends over time that correlate predicate violations with increased likelihood of failure.

Software tomography as realized through the GAMMA system [5] shares our goal of low-overhead distributed monitoring of deployed code. Applications to date have focused on code coverage and traditional performance monitoring tasks, whereas our primary interest is bug isolation. Our strategy uses randomization within a single instrumented binary, while GAMMA emphasizes choices in initial probe placement and iterative refinement over time. Our earlier discussion of statically selective sampling (see Sect. 2.3.7) suggests that these two considerations are complementary. It is also worth noting that our predicates do indirectly yield coverage information: given fair sampling, the sum of all predicate counters at a site converges on the true relative coverage of that site.

Efforts to directly apply statistical modeling principles to debugging have met with mixed results. Early work in this area by Burnell and Horvitz [8] uses program slicing in conjunction with Bayesian belief networks to filter and rank the possible causes for a given bug. Empirical evaluation shows that the slicing component alone finds 65% of bug causes, while the probabilistic model correctly identifies another 10%. This additional payoff may seem small in light of the effort, measured in multiple man-years, required to distill experts' often tacit knowledge into a formal belief network. However, the approach does illustrate one strategy for integrating information about program structure into the statistical modeling process.

In more recent work, Podgurski et al. [53] apply statistical feature selection, clustering, and multivariate visualization techniques to the task of classifying software failure reports. The intent is to bucket each report into an equivalence group believed to share the same underlying cause. Features are derived offline from fine-grained execution traces without sampling; this approach reduces the noise level of the data but greatly restricts the instrumentation schemes that are practical to deploy outside of a controlled testing environment. As in our own earlier work, Podgurski uses logistic regression to select features that are highly predictive of failure. Clustering tends to identify small, tight groups of runs that do share a single cause but that are not always maximal. That is, one cause may be split across several clusters.

In contrast, current industrial practice uses stack traces to cluster failure reports into equivalence classes. Two crash reports showing the same stack trace, or perhaps only the same top-of-stack function, are presumed to be two reports of the same failure. This heuristic works to the extent that a single cause corresponds to a single point of failure, but our experience with MOSS, RHYTHMBOX, and EXIF suggests that this assumption may not often hold. In MOSS, we find that only bugs #2 and #5 have truly unique "signature" stacks: a crash location that is present if and only if the corresponding bug was actually triggered. These bugs are also our most deterministic. Bugs #4 and #6 also have nearly unique stack signatures. The remaining bugs are much less consistent: each stack signature is observed after a variety of different bugs, and each triggered bug causes failure in a variety of different stack states. RHYTHMBOX and EXIF bugs caused crashes so long after the bad behavior that stacks were of limited use or no use at all.

For some highly available systems, even a single failure must be avoided. Once the behaviors that predict imminent failure are known, automatic corrective measures may be able to prevent the failure from occurring at all. The Software Dependability Framework (SDF) [26] uses multivariate state estimation techniques to model and thereby predict impending system failures. Instrumentation is assumed to be complete and is typically domain-specific.

Studies that attempt real-world deployment of monitored software must address a host of practical engineering concerns, from distribution to installation to user support to data collection and warehousing. Elbaum and Hardojo [17, 18] have reported on a limited deployment of instrumented Pine binaries. Their experiences have helped to guide our own design of a wide public deployment of applications with sampled instrumentation, presently underway [40].

6

Conclusion

> *Beware of bugs in the above code; I have only proved it correct, not tried it.*
>
> –Donald Knuth, *"Notes on the van Emde Boas construction of priority deques: An instructive use of recursion"*

It is an unfortunate fact that essentially all deployed software systems have bugs, and that users often encounter these bugs. The resources (measured in time, money, or people) available for improving software are always limited.

Widespread Internet connectivity makes possible a radical change to this situation. For the first time it is feasible to directly observe the reality of a software system's deployment. Through sheer numbers, the user community brings far more resources to bear on exercising a piece of software than could possibly be provided by the software's authors. Coupled with an instrumentation, reporting, and analysis infrastructure, these users can potentially replace guesswork with real triage, directing scarce engineering resources to those areas that benefit the most people.

The Cooperative Bug Isolation project represents one effort to leverage the strength in these users' numbers. We have designed, developed, and deployed a debugging support system that encompasses a complete feedback loop from source to users to feedback to bug fixes.

In terms of the original goals of this research, CBI is a qualified success. Our instrumentation strategy provides fair, randomly sampled data suitable for use with a wide range of statistical analyses. The sampling transformation is quite general, and may be of independent interest in areas beyond just bug hunting. For CPU-intensive applications such as performance benchmarks, our current implementation requires exclusion of bottleneck code in order to limit overhead. However there is room for improvement. Similar sampling schemes described in Chap. 5, especially those by Chilimbi et al., have achieved very low overheads. The path balancing optimization, proposed in Sect. 2.3.6 but not yet implemented, leaves the fast path almost entirely instrumentation free and thereby should significantly improve performance. We have not pursued performance optimizations further in this work because the current system is good enough for the applications we have looked at so far, both in controlled case studies and in our public deployment.

The engineering challenge of creating a deployable system has been met. The public deployment is, in a word, real. It includes instrumented binaries ready to download and install, polished user interfaces, a secure feedback collection server, and a community of end users who trust and use our code every day. This user com-

B. Liblit: Cooperative Bug Isolation, LNCS 4440, pp. 95–96, 2007.
© Springer-Verlag Berlin Heidelberg 2007

munity is not yet large enough to drive our statistical bug isolation algorithms; research of this kind is inherently difficult in an academic environment. Nevertheless, we feel it has been a valuable exercise to push the entire system forward to the point where it was ready to face the public at all. Our experience with the public deployment gives us much greater confidence that a system like the one we propose is practical and viable.

Lastly, the statistical debugging techniques we have described show that one can actually find and fix bugs with sparsely sampled data. At the outset of this project it was unclear just how little information one could get away with. We have successfully isolated single bugs and multiple bugs; deterministic bugs and nondeterministic bugs; bugs in batch-oriented systems and bugs in multi-threaded interactive systems; known bugs seeded in known code and previously unknown bugs discovered in code unfamiliar to the CBI team. We believe that statistical debugging based on automated user feedback has the potential to be a valuable addition to the software engineer's bug hunting repertoire.

References

1. Jennifer M. Anderson, Lance M. Berc, Jeffrey Dean, Sanjay Ghemawat, Monika R. Henzinger, Shun-Tak A. Leung, Richard L. Sites, Mark T. Vandevoorde, Carl A. Waldspurger, and William E. Weihl. Continuous profiling: Where have all the cycles gone? *ACM Transactions on Computer Systems*, 15(4):357–390, November 1997.
2. Matthew Arnold and Barbara Ryder. A framework for reducing the cost of instrumented code. *ACM SIGPLAN Notices*, 36(5):168–179, May 2001.
3. Matthew Arnold and Peter F. Sweeney. Approximating the calling context tree via sampling. Research report RC 21789 (98099), IBM T.J. Watson Research Center, Yorktown Heights, New York, July 7 2000.
4. Thomas Ball and James R. Larus. Efficient path profiling. In *Proceedings of the 29th Annual International Symposium on Microarchitecture*, pages 46–57. ACM Press, 1996.
5. Jim Bowring, Alessandro Orso, and Mary Jean Harrold. Monitoring deployed software using software tomography. In Matthew B. Dwyer, editor, *Proceedings of the 2002 ACM SIGPLAN-SIGSOFT workshop on Program Analysis for Software Tools and Engineering (PASTE-02)*, volume 28, 1 of *SOFTWARE ENGINEERING NOTES*, pages 2–9. ACM Press, 2002.
6. Leo Breiman, J. H. Friedman, R. A. Olshen, and C. J. Stone. *Classification and Regression Trees*. Statistics/Probability Series. Wadsworth Publishing Company, Belmont, California, U.S.A., 1984.
7. Pete Broadwell, Matt Harren, and Naveen Sastry. Scrash: A system for generating secure crash information. In *Proceedings of the 12th Usenix Security Symposium*, pages 273–284, August 2003.
8. Lisa Burnell and Eric Horvitz. Structure and chance: melding logic and probability for software debugging. *Communications of the ACM*, 38(3):31–41, 57, March 1995.
9. Michael Burrows, Ulfar Erlingson, Shun-Tak Leung, Mark Vandevoorde, Carl Waldspurger, Kip Walker, and Bill Weihl. Efficient and flexible value sampling. *ACM SIGPLAN Notices*, 35(11):160–167, November 2000.
10. John Canny. Collaborative filtering with privacy. In *Proceedings of the IEEE Symposium on Research in Security and Privacy*, pages 45–57, Oakland, CA, May 2002. IEEE Computer Society, Technical Committee on Security and Privacy, IEEE Computer Society Press.
11. Martin Christopher Carlisle. *Olden: Parallelizing Programs with Dynamic Data Structures on Distributed-Memory Machines*. PhD thesis, Department of Computer Science, Princeton University, June 1996.

12. Trishul Chilimbi and Mattias Hauswirth. Low-overhead memory leak detection using adaptive statistical profiling. In *ASPLOS: Eleventh International Conference on Architectural Support for Programming Languages and Operating Systems*, Boston, MA, October 2004.

13. Chrysanthos Dellarocas. Immunizing online reputation reporting systems against unfair ratings and discriminatory behavior. In *Proceedings of the 2nd ACM Conference on Electronic Commerce (EC-00)*, pages 150–157. ACM, 2000.

14. Brian Demsky and Martin C. Rinard. Role-based exploration of object-oriented programs. In *Proceedings of the International Conference on Software Engineering*, Buenos Aires, Argentina, May 2002. Association for Computing Machinery.

15. Nii Dodoo, Lee Lin, and Michael D. Ernst. Selecting, refining, and evaluating predicates for program analysis. Technical Report MIT-LCS-TR-914, MIT Laboratory for Computer Science, Cambridge, MA, July 21 2003.

16. Andrew Edwards, Amitabh Srivastava, and Hoi Vo. Vulcan: Binary transformation in a distributed environment. Technical Report MSR-TR-2001-50, Microsoft Research (MSR), April 2001.

17. Sebastian Elbaum and Madeline Hardojo. Deploying instrumented software to assist the testing activity. In Orso and Porter [50], pages 31–33.

18. Sebastian G. Elbaum and Madeline Hardojo. An empirical study of profiling strategies for released software and their impact on testing activities. In George S. Avrunin and Gregg Rothermel, editors, *Proceedings of the ACM/SIGSOFT International Symposium on Software Testing and Analysis (ISSTA 2004)*, pages 65–75, Boston, MA, July 11–14 2004. ACM.

19. Michael Ernst, Jake Cockrell, William G. Griswold, and David Notkin. Dynamically discovering likely program invariants to support program evolution. In *Proceedings of the 21st International Conference on Software Engineering*, pages 213–225. ACM Press, May 1999.

20. Michael D. Ernst, Jake Cockrell, William G. Griswold, and David Notkin. Dynamically discovering likely program invariants to support program evolution. *IEEE Transactions on Software Engineering*, 27(2):1–25, February 2001.

21. David Esler. Welcome to the virtual ramp. *Overhaul & Maintenance*, VII(2):55, March 2001.

22. Cormac Flanagan, K. Rustan M. Leino, Mark Lillibridge, Greg Nelson, James B. Saxe, and Raymie Stata. Extended static checking for Java. In Cindy Norris and Jr. James B. Fenwick, editors, *Proceedings of the ACM SIGPLAN 2002 Conference on Programming Language Design and Implementation (PLDI-02)*, volume 37, 5 of *ACM SIGPLAN Notices*, pages 234–245. ACM Press, 2002.

23. The GNOME Project. *GObject Reference Manual*, GLib 2.4.3 edition, June 2004. available at <http://developer.gnome.org/doc/API/2.0/gobject/index.html>.

24. T. R. Golub, D. K. Slonim, P. Tamayo, C. Huard, M. Gaasenbeek, J. P. Mesirov, H. Coller, M. L. Loh, J. R. Downing, M. A. Caligiuri, C. D. Bloomfield, and E. S. Lander. Molecular classification of cancer: class discovery and class prediction by gene expression monitoring. *Science*, 286(5439):531–537, 1999.

25. Carl Gould, Zhendong Su, and Premkumar Devanbu. Static checking of dynamically generated queries in database applications. In *Proceedings of the 26th International Conference on Software Engineering*, pages 645–654. IEEE Computer Society, 2004.

26. Kenny C. Gross, Scott McMaster, Adam Porter, Aleskey Urmanov, and Lawrence G. Votta. Proactive system maintenance using software telemetry. In Orso and Porter [50], pages 24–26.

27. Sudheendra Hangal and Monica S. Lam. Tracking down software bugs using automatic anomaly detection. In *Proceedings of the 24th International Conference on Software Engineering (ICSE-02)*, pages 291–301. ACM Press, 2002.
28. T. Hastie, R. Tibshirani, and J. Friedman. *The Elements of Statistical Learning*. Stats. Springer, 2001.
29. Herbert Hecht and Patrick Crane. Rare conditions and their effect on software failures. In *Reliability and Maintainability Symposium*, pages 334–337, Anaheim, California, USA, 1994.
30. Herbert Hecht, Myron Hecht, and Dolores R. Wallace. Toward more effective testing for high-assurance systems. In *Proceedings of the 2nd High-Assurance Systems Engineering Workshop*, pages 176–181. IEEE Computer Society, 1997.
31. Thomas A. Henzinger, Ranjit Jhala, Rupak Majumdar, and Gregoire Sutre. Lazy abstraction. In Norris and James B. Fenwick [49], pages 58–70.
32. Martin Hirzel and Trishul Chilimbi. Bursty tracing: A framework for low-overhead temporal profiling, November 24 2001.
33. Gerard J. Holzmann. Economics of software verification. In ACM, editor, *ACM SIGPLAN–SIGSOFT workshop on Program Analysis for Software Tools and Engineering*, pages 80–89, New York, NY, USA, June 18–19 2001. ACM Press. Invited talk.
34. IEEE Standards Committee 754. *IEEE Standard for binary floating-point arithmetic, ANSI/IEEE Standard 754-1985*. Institute of Electrical and Electronics Engineers, New York, 1985. Reprinted in ACM SIGPLAN Notices, 22(2):9-25, 1987.
35. Intel Corp. *Instruction Set Reference*, volume 2 of *IA-32 Intel Architecture Software Developer's Manual*. Intel Corp., Mt. Prospect, Illinois, 2001.
36. International Organization for Standardization. *ISO/IEC 9899:1999: Programming Languages — C*. International Organization for Standardization, Geneva, Switzerland, December 1999. Available in electronic form for online purchase at <http://webstore.ansi.org/> and <http://www.cssinfo.com/>.
37. Rob Johnson and David Wagner. Finding user/kernel pointer bugs with type inference. In *Proceedings of the 11th USENIX Security Symposium*. USENIX, August 2004.
38. E.L. Lehmann. *Testing Statistical Hypotheses*. John Wiley & Sons, 2nd edition, 1986.
39. Ben Liblit. The Cooperative Bug Isolation Project. <http://www.cs.wisc.edu/cbi/>.
40. Ben Liblit, Mayur Naik, Alice X. Zheng, Alex Aiken, and Michael I. Jordan. Public deployment of Cooperative Bug Isolation. In Alessandro Orso and Adam Porter, editors, *Proceedings of the Second International Workshop on Remote Analysis and Measurement of Software Systems (RAMSS '04)*, pages 57–62, Edinburgh, Scotland, May 24 2004.
41. John Markoff. Microsoft reports progress in averting computer crashes. *The New York Times*, page C.7, October 3 2002.
42. Microsoft Corp. Microsoft 2002 annual report and form 10-K. Available at <http://www.microsoft.com/msft/ar02/>, Redmond, Washington, 2002.
43. Barton Miller, David Koski, Cjin Pheow Lee, Vivekananda Maganty, Ravi Murthy, Ajitkumar Natarajan, and Jeff Steidl. Fuzz revisited: A re-examination of the reliability of UNIX utilities and services. Technical report, Computer Science Department, University of Wisconsin, Madison, WI, 1995.
44. Mozilla.org. Mozilla bug database. <http://bugzilla.mozilla.org/>, December 1 2006.
45. Mozilla.org. Mozilla Talkback reports. <http://talkback-public.mozilla.org/reports/>, December 1 2006.
46. Louis Naugès. Réalité des usages des PC en entreprises. Available at <http://www.microcost.com/fr/?Actualités>, September 2004.

47. George Necula, Scott McPeak, and Westley Weimer. CCURED: Type-safe retrofitting of legacy code. In Norris and James B. Fenwick [49], pages 128–139.

48. George C. Necula, Scott McPeak, Shree Prakash Rahul, and Westley Weimer. CIL: Intermediate language and tools for analysis and transformation of C programs. In R. Nigel Horspool, editor, *Compiler Construction, 11th International Conference, CC 2002, held as part of the Joint European Conferences on Theory and Practice of Software, ETAPS 2002, Proceedings*, volume 2304 of *Lecture Notes in Computer Science*, pages 213–228, Grenoble, France, April 8–12 2002. Springer.

49. Cindy Norris and Jr. James B. Fenwick, editors. *Proceedings of the 2002 ACM SIGPLAN-SIGACT Symposium on Principles of Programming Languages (POPL-02)*, volume 37, 1 of *ACM SIGPLAN Notices*. ACM Press, 2002.

50. Alessandro Orso and Adam Porter, editors. *RAMSS '03: 1st International Workshop on Remote Analysis and Measurement of Software Systems*, Portland, Oregon, May 9 2003.

51. Thomas J. Ostrand, Elaine J. Weyuker, and Robert M. Bell. Where the bugs are. In *Proceedings of the 2004 ACM SIGSOFT International Symposium on Software Testing and Analysis*, pages 86–96. ACM Press, 2004.

52. Randy Pausch. An academic's field guide to Electronic Arts. Available at <http://www.andrew.cmu.edu/user/tshah/PauschAcademicsFieldGuideToEA.pdf>, October 2004.

53. Andy Podgurski, David Leon, Patrick Francis, Wes Masri, Melinda Minch, Jiayang Sun, and Bin Wang. Automated support for classifying software failure reports. In *Proceedings of the 25th International Conference on Software Engineering (ICSE-03)*, pages 465–477. IEEE Computer Society, 2003.

54. Brock Pytlik, Manos Renieris, Shriram Krishnamurthi, and Steven P. Reiss. Automated fault localization using potential invariants. In Michiel Ronsse and Koen De Bosschere, editors, *AADEBUG 2003: Fifth International Workshop on Automated and Algorithmic Debugging*, pages 273–276, Ghent, Belgium, September 8–10 2003.

55. S. P. Reiss and M. Renieris. Encoding program executions. In *Proceedings of the 23rd International Conference on Software Engineering*, pages 221–230. IEEE Computer Society Press, May 2001.

56. Saul Schleimer, Daniel S. Wilkerson, and Alex Aiken. Winnowing: local algorithms for document fingerprinting. In ACM, editor, *Proceedings of the 2003 ACM SIGMOD International Conference on Management of Data 2003, San Diego, California, June 09–12, 2003*, pages 76–85, New York, NY 10036, USA, 2003. ACM Press.

57. SPEC 95. Standard Performance Evaluation Corporation Benchmarks. <http://www.spec.org/osg/cpu95/CINT95/>, July 1995.

58. Robert Tibshirani, Trevor Hastie, Balasubramanian Narasimhan, and Gilbert Chu. Diagnosis of multiple cancer types by shrunken centroids of gene expression. *Proceedings of the National Academy of Sciences of the United States of America*, 99(10):6567–6572, 2002.

59. Omri Traub, Stuart Schechter, and Michael D. Smith. Ephemeral instrumentation for lightweight program profiling. Unpublished technical report, Department of Electrical Engineering and Computer Science, Hardward University, Cambridge, Massachusetts, June 2000.

60. Dennis M. Volpano and Geoffrey Smith. A type-based approach to program security. In Michel Bidoit and Max Dauchet, editors, *TAPSOFT '97: Theory and Practice of Software Development*, volume 1214 of *Lecture Notes in Computer Science*, pages 607–621. Springer-Verlag, 1997.

61. John Whaley. A portable sampling-based profiler for Java virtual machines. In *Proceedings of the ACM 2000 conference on Java Grande*, pages 78–87. ACM Press, 2000.

62. John H. William, Alexander Aiken, and Edward L. Wimmers. Program transformation in the presence of errors. In ACM, editor, *POPL '90. Proceedings of the seventeenth annual ACM symposium on Principles of programming languages, January 17–19, 1990, San Francisco, CA*, pages 210–217, New York, NY, USA, 1990. ACM Press.

63. Annie T. T. Ying, Gail C. Murphy, Raymond Ng, and Mark C. Chu-Carroll. Predicting source code changes by mining change history. *IEEE Trans. Softw. Eng.*, 30(9):574–586, 2004.

64. Steve Zdancewic, Lantian Zheng, Nathaniel Nystrom, and Andrew C. Myers. Untrusted hosts and confidentiality: Secure program partitioning. In *Proceedings of the 18th ACM Symposium on Operating Systems Principles (SOSP'01)*, pages 1–14, Chateau Lake Louise, Banff, Alberta, Canada, October 2001. Appeared as ACM Operating Systems Review 35.5.

65. Alice X. Zheng, Michael I. Jordan, Ben Liblit, and Alex Aiken. Statistical debugging of sampled programs. In Sebastian Thrun, Lawrence Saul, and Bernhard Schölkopf, editors, *Advances in Neural Information Processing Systems 16*. MIT Press, Cambridge, MA, 2004.

66. Thomas Zimmermann, Peter Weißgerber, Stephan Diehl, and Andreas Zeller. Mining version histories to guide software changes. In *Proceedings of the 26th International Conference on Software Engineering*, pages 563–572. IEEE Computer Society, 2004.

Lecture Notes in Computer Science

For information about Vols. 1–4349

please contact your bookseller or Springer

Vol. 4400: J.F. Peters, A. Skowron, V.W. Marek, E. Orłowska, R. Słowinski, W. Ziarko (Eds.), Transactions on Rough Sets VII, Part II. X, 381 pages. 2007.

Vol. 4399: T. Kovacs, X. Llorà, K. Takadama, P.L. Lanzi, W. Stolzmann, S.W. Wilson (Eds.), Learning Classifier Systems. XII, 345 pages. 2007. (Sublibrary LNAI).

Vol. 4398: S. Marchand-Maillet, E. Bruno, A. Nürnberger, M. Detyniecki (Eds.), Adaptive Multimedia Retrieval: User, Context, and Feedback. XI, 269 pages. 2007.

Vol. 4397: C. Stephanidis, M. Pieper (Eds.), Universal Access in Ambient Intelligence Environments. XV, 467 pages. 2007.

Vol. 4396: J. García-Vidal, L. Cerdà-Alabern (Eds.), Wireless Systems and Mobility in Next Generation Internet. IX, 271 pages. 2007.

Vol. 4395: M. Daydé, J.M.L.M. Palma, Á.L.G.A. Coutinho, E. Pacitti, J.C. Lopes (Eds.), High Performance Computing for Computational Science - VECPAR 2006. XXIV, 721 pages. 2007.

Vol. 4394: A. Gelbukh (Ed.), Computational Linguistics and Intelligent Text Processing. XVI, 648 pages. 2007.

Vol. 4393: W. Thomas, P. Weil (Eds.), STACS 2007. XVIII, 708 pages. 2007.

Vol. 4392: S.P. Vadhan (Ed.), Theory of Cryptography. XI, 595 pages. 2007.

Vol. 4391: Y. Stylianou, M. Faundez-Zanuy, A. Esposito (Eds.), Progress in Nonlinear Speech Processing. XII, 269 pages. 2007.

Vol. 4390: S.O. Kuznetsov, S. Schmidt (Eds.), Formal Concept Analysis. X, 329 pages. 2007. (Sublibrary LNAI).

Vol. 4389: D. Weyns, H.V.D. Parunak, F. Michel (Eds.), Environments for Multi-Agent Systems III. X, 273 pages. 2007. (Sublibrary LNAI).

Vol. 4385: K. Coninx, K. Luyten, K.A. Schneider (Eds.), Task Models and Diagrams for Users Interface Design. XI, 355 pages. 2007.

Vol. 4384: T. Washio, K. Satoh, H. Takeda, A. Inokuchi (Eds.), New Frontiers in Artificial Intelligence. IX, 401 pages. 2007. (Sublibrary LNAI).

Vol. 4383: E. Bin, A. Ziv, S. Ur (Eds.), Hardware and Software, Verification and Testing. XII, 235 pages. 2007.

Vol. 4381: J. Akiyama, W.Y.C. Chen, M. Kano, X. Li, Q. Yu (Eds.), Discrete Geometry, Combinatorics and Graph Theory. XI, 289 pages. 2007.

Vol. 4380: S. Spaccapietra, P. Atzeni, F. Fages, M.-S. Hacid, M. Kifer, J. Mylopoulos, B. Pernici, P. Shvaiko, J. Trujillo, I. Zaihrayeu (Eds.), Journal on Data Semantics VIII. XV, 219 pages. 2007.

Vol. 4379: M. Südholt, C. Consel (Eds.), Object-Oriented Technology. VIII, 157 pages. 2007.

Vol. 4378: I. Virbitskaite, A. Voronkov (Eds.), Perspectives of Systems Informatics. XIV, 496 pages. 2007.

Vol. 4377: M. Abe (Ed.), Topics in Cryptology – CT-RSA 2007. XI, 403 pages. 2006.

Vol. 4376: E. Frachtenberg, U. Schwiegelshohn (Eds.), Job Scheduling Strategies for Parallel Processing. VII, 257 pages. 2007.

Vol. 4374: J.F. Peters, A. Skowron, I. Düntsch, J. Grzymała-Busse, E. Orłowska, L. Polkowski (Eds.), Transactions on Rough Sets VI, Part I. XII, 499 pages. 2007.

Vol. 4373: K. Langendoen, T. Voigt (Eds.), Wireless Sensor Networks. XIII, 358 pages. 2007.

Vol. 4372: M. Kaufmann, D. Wagner (Eds.), Graph Drawing. XIV, 454 pages. 2007.

Vol. 4371: K. Inoue, K. Satoh, F. Toni (Eds.), Computational Logic in Multi-Agent Systems. X, 315 pages. 2007. (Sublibrary LNAI).

Vol. 4370: P.P Lévy, B. Le Grand, F. Poulet, M. Soto, L. Darago, L. Toubiana, J.-F. Vibert (Eds.), Pixelization Paradigm. XV, 279 pages. 2007.

Vol. 4369: M. Umeda, A. Wolf, O. Bartenstein, U. Geske, D. Seipel, O. Takata (Eds.), Declarative Programming for Knowledge Management. X, 229 pages. 2006. (Sublibrary LNAI).

Vol. 4368: T. Erlebach, C. Kaklamanis (Eds.), Approximation and Online Algorithms. X, 345 pages. 2007.

Vol. 4367: K. De Bosschere, D. Kaeli, P. Stenström, D. Whalley, T. Ungerer (Eds.), High Performance Embedded Architectures and Compilers. XI, 307 pages. 2007.

Vol. 4366: K. Tuyls, R. Westra, Y. Saeys, A. Nowé (Eds.), Knowledge Discovery and Emergent Complexity in Bioinformatics. IX, 183 pages. 2007. (Sublibrary LNBI).

Vol. 4364: T. Kühne (Ed.), Models in Software Engineering. XI, 332 pages. 2007.

Vol. 4362: J. van Leeuwen, G.F. Italiano, W. van der Hoek, C. Meinel, H. Sack, F. Plášil (Eds.), SOFSEM 2007: Theory and Practice of Computer Science. XXI, 937 pages. 2007.

Vol. 4361: H.J. Hoogeboom, G. Păun, G. Rozenberg, A. Salomaa (Eds.), Membrane Computing. IX, 555 pages. 2006.

Vol. 4360: W. Dubitzky, A. Schuster, P.M.A. Sloot, M. Schroeder, M. Romberg (Eds.), Distributed, High-Performance and Grid Computing in Computational Biology. X, 192 pages. 2007. (Sublibrary LNBI).

Vol. 4358: R. Vidal, A. Heyden, Y. Ma (Eds.), Dynamical Vision. IX, 329 pages. 2007.

Vol. 4357: L. Buttyán, V. Gligor, D. Westhoff (Eds.), Security and Privacy in Ad-Hoc and Sensor Networks. X, 193 pages. 2006.

Vol. 4355: J. Julliand, O. Kouchnarenko (Eds.), B 2007: Formal Specification and Development in B. XIII, 293 pages. 2006.

Vol. 4354: M. Hanus (Ed.), Practical Aspects of Declarative Languages. X, 335 pages. 2006.

Vol. 4353: T. Schwentick, D. Suciu (Eds.), Database Theory – ICDT 2007. XI, 419 pages. 2006.

Vol. 4352: T.-J. Cham, J. Cai, C. Dorai, D. Rajan, T.-S. Chua, L.-T. Chia (Eds.), Advances in Multimedia Modeling, Part II. XVIII, 743 pages. 2006.

Vol. 4351: T.-J. Cham, J. Cai, C. Dorai, D. Rajan, T.-S. Chua, L.-T. Chia (Eds.), Advances in Multimedia Modeling, Part I. XIX, 797 pages. 2006.